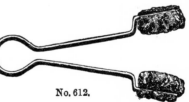
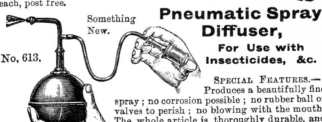

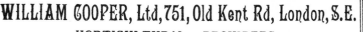

WILLIAM COOPER, Ltd, 751, Old Kent Rd, London, S.E.

HORTICULTURAL PROVIDERS.

Flower Gatherer.

No. 628. Superior Make, 3s. each.

Pruner.

No. 629.

Best Quality.
2s. 6d. each.

Vine.

Best Make, 2s. 6d. each.

No. 630.

Weeding Fork.

No. 631.
Polished Handle and Self
Bright, 5in.
PRICE 6d. each; 5s. per doz.

Garden Trowel.

No. 632.
Blue Japanned, 6in. Polished Handle.
PRICE 5d. each; 4s. per doz.

Glazier's Knife.

No. 633.

Best
Make.
PRICE
9d. ea.

FERTILO

HARVEY'S UNIVERSAL FERTILIZER

A Stimulating Food for all Plants

Invigorating
Lasting
Safe
Clean
Cheap

Testimonials
Press
Opinions
on
other side.

At
Shrewsbury
GREAT
SHOW
1904
one
Exhibitor
WON
· 15 ·
PRIZES
by using
FERTILO

The Fertilizer for the
AMATEUR and
the PROFESSIONAL
GARDENER.

Manufactured:
J. R. HARVEY & CO.,
KIDDERMINSTER.

BLAKE & MACKENZIE, LIVERPOOL.

THE
EDWARDIAN
GARDENER'S GUIDE

FOR ALL GARDEN LOVERS

• OLD HOUSE •

Published in Great Britain in 2014 by Old House books & maps
c/o Osprey Publishing, PO Box 883, Oxford OX2 9PH, UK.
c/o Osprey Publishing, PO Box 3985, New York, NY 10185-3985, USA.
Website: www.oldhousebooks.co.uk

A CIP catalogue record for this book is available from the British Library.

ISBN-13: 978 1 90840 288 2

Extracts from 'One & All Garden Books' originally published in 1913 by the Agricultural and
Horticultural Association, London.

Printed in China through World Print Ltd.

IMAGE ACKNOWLEDGEMENTS
The Garden Museum, pages 1, 2, 3, 4, 20, 25, 28, 29, 39, 44, 45, 48, 58, 62, 63, 64, 65, 68, 69,
73, 74, 80, 86, 92, 93, 104, 105, 110, 112, 120, 121, 125, 146, 147, 148; Mary Evans Picture
Library, pages 8, 12, 32, 54, 89, 96, 142

All other illustrations are from the original One & All Garden Books.

14 15 16 17 18   10 9 8 7 6 5 4 3 2 1

Much of the material reproduced in this book was first published in 1913, and contains the
common spelling and terms used in everyday language of that period.

❧ CONTENTS ❧

Part I: Types of Garden

Part II: The Flower Garden

Part III: The Allotment and Vegetable Plot

Pl. XXIII

AMARYLLIS *spatha multiflora corollis campanulatis marginibus reflexis genitalibus declinatis.*

Published according to Act by F. Miller June 1755

Introduction

by Twigs Way

The 'One & All Garden Books' were produced by the London branch of the Agricultural and Horticultural Association in the first decade of the twentieth century, and sold for a penny. Edited by the social reformer Edward Owen Greening (1836–1923), they arose out of the working class cooperative movements that sought to better the life of the rural and urban labourer and his family. The association – originally founded in the mid-nineteenth century, and counting the art critic John Ruskin amongst its founders – claimed to circulate three million publications every year, and to sell, at a minimal profit, fifteen million packets of 'cheap reliable seeds, bearing clear cultural directions'. What profits were made were invested back into schemes for public benefit, including the founding of local horticultural associations. Greening, who was himself a Fellow of the Royal Horticultural Society, commissioned the foremost garden writers of the period to pen a series of booklets on the most popular gardening topics of the period. Starting with 'Sweet Peas', at the time perhaps the most popular garden flower of the working classes, the series grew to include forty booklets ranging across topics from allotments and antirrhinums to weather and window gardens. Each booklet was sold for one penny or, for five shillings a year, a subscriber could be sent all the publications as well as samples of seeds, fertilisers etc, which were also produced and sold by the Association. The popularity of the series is attested by the reprinting of several editions of some of the topics – 'Perennials' (booklet No. 5), for example, went to at least five editions, and 'Asters' reached six editions, indicating sales of both in the region of 200,000 copies (around 40,000 copies were generally made of a first edition).

Topics covered by the booklets give an insight into both the central concerns of the Association and the social and horticultural context of the period, as well as reflecting the fashion in plants and planting styles. Food production for the family runs through several of the booklets, whether on the allotment or in the garden, and as well as individual booklets on these subjects a 'special' two-part booklet dealt with the planting and cropping of allotments generally. Reference was made to the allotment 'movement' that was still at that date trying to ensure provision for all, as well as provision of allotment plots for gardeners and soldiers close to barracks. Many of the booklets refer to the growing urbanisation of the early twentieth century: tackling problems with small gardens, shady lawns, small greenhouses (an aspiration for many) or, for the most restricted, window gardens, indoor gardens, and even the growing of mushrooms in cellars. From 1893 onwards Greening himself lived in Lewisham (South London), and he brought to bear his own experience in several of the topics. 'Shady Gardens', for example, included an image of the editor's garden, although rather larger in scale than the narrow back garden of a terraced house shown on the previous page in the same publication.

The coming of the electric trams allowing people to move away from the slums, the creation of 'pretty garden suburbs' for the middle classes, and to a lesser extent garden cities for labourers at the new manufactories, were all cited as playing their part in the rise of gardening for all. Into the small spaces allotted to the working- and even middle-class gardener were packed the most popular flowers of the day, often planted not only for their cheering influence but also for competition in the popular shows that sprung up in both rural and urban areas. Phlox, pansies, carnations, annual or China asters, antirrhinums, stocks, and sweet peas each had a booklet to themselves, whilst other more general booklets dealt with annuals (popular because of their cheapness), climbers and perennials. For the more adventurous rockeries, ferneries and even grottoes, could be created, and hints were given on layout and design.

In the pages of the 'One & All Garden Books' gardening was to be society's salvation and England's triumph. The English lawn is described as having a superiority which will 'ever remain unchallenged', the raising of perennials from seed as 'a hobby with ample room for the enterprising spirit', and the blossoming of window gardens 'an important act of local patriotism'. The phraseology and approach are redolent of that moment in time when Victorian aspirations met with Edwardian achievement, that golden period before the First World War – when the flower garden was to be cast aside and the growing of the nation's food became a matter of heroism rather than an innocent hobby.

There is much that is familiar in the pages reproduced here from the original 'One & All' booklets. Concern with soil preparation, planting times, the discouragement and extermination of pests, and the constant striving for the best of gardens despite the unpredictability of the English weather. But there is also much that is of the past. The use of 'soil fumigant' to rid the lawn of worms by wholesale slaughter, the promotion of the popular Wardian case to enable fern culture in the gloomiest of early Edwardian living rooms, the ongoing fight for the right to an allotment, and of course the ease with which horse manure might be obtained by merely going out onto a busy street. Advertisements too evoke a world at once similar and strange: grass seed and plant labels, Bordeaux Mix, Pears Soap and Jeyes Fluid share pages with exhortations to 'take up fretwork' as a fascinating evening hobby, invest in Canary Guano, smoke Players Cigarettes or spray concentrated nicotine through the greenhouse. The past may be a foreign country but for the gardener it is in many ways an instantly recognisable one.

━━━◅◅◅►►►━━━

NOTE: Some of the plants and chemicals recommended in the 'One & All' books are no longer in use. Particular notice is drawn to the fact that it is illegal to plant (or spread in any way) Polygonum cuspidatum (Japanese Knotweed) and Impatiens glandulifera (Himalayan balsam). In addition, arsenic, nicotine sprays, and uncontrolled garden/allotment use of Jeyes Fluid, once all common pest control methods, are now illegal.

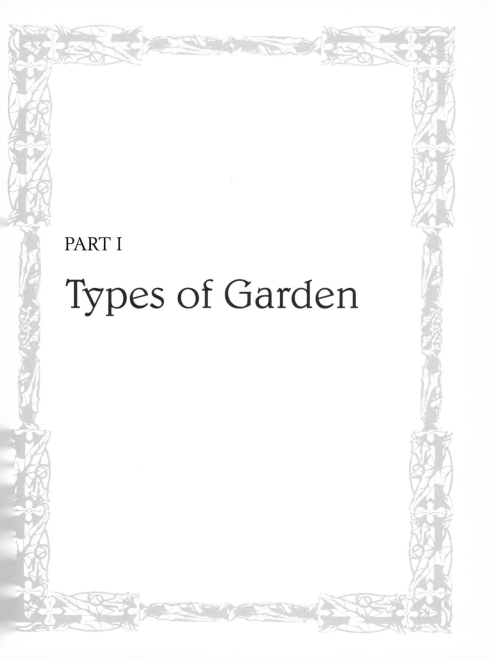

PART I

Types of Garden

PART I

Types of Garden

In the modern imagination the Edwardian garden is one of expansive lawns, overflowing borders and rich shrubberies. But in reality the vast majority of gardens were small, belonging to the newly suburbanised middle and working classes. In the booklet on 'Small Gardens' (No. 26 in the series) these are defined as anything from 10 feet wide and 20-30 feet long up to the rarer quarter of an acre. In these gardens flower borders had to be crimped to between a foot long and four foot wide, and the confining fences and walls formed a constant backdrop. Strict economy dictated use of clinker or flints as edging, with larger broken bricks for paths or a simple 'rockery'. Despite these restrictions a mix of annuals and perennials (all grown from the One & All seed supplies) could create 'a suburban paradise', supplemented with hanging baskets, window boxes and trellises. Shade was no limiter of such endeavours, with recommendations for suitable plants, including the ever-popular 'ferny grot' and more invasive garden plants, such as Japanese knotweed (now banned). Lawns were only suitable for the medium sized garden, but here lavish attention was paid to their cultivation. A 'lawn mowing machine' was only used after good growth had been established, and previous to that the old-fashioned scythe was still recommended. Rolling should be frequent and 'ill weeds' had no place on an 'English lawn'! Perhaps the most fascinating in this section however are the recommendations and illustrations for the window gardens and indoor gardens which were so beloved in an age when backyards had frequently to be given over to the coal house and the outdoor privy. These gardens also had a special meaning for the 'indwellers' of the house: in the words of Greening, 'the wife and daughters, tied much indoors by the endless engrossing cares of house duties', or the invalid, trapped in a sunless room. Even a pot of ivy in the hearth, or an acorn grown in a bottle, would bring cheer. The lack of sunlight in such rooms must in some cases have been brought about by the effusive window boxes, the scale and magnificence of which threatened to totally obscure the actual window. Trailing nasturtium combined with tall stocks, bushy pelargonium, petunias and the popular tropaeolum created masses of foliage, which not only added beauty to the dwellings and pleasure to the inhabitants but, as the writer optimistically claimed, led to increased commercial prosperity of entire areas.

Twigs Way

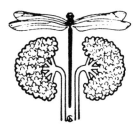

A Foreword by the Editor

THE subject of Small Gardens is happily becoming one of national importance. Our towns and cities are being transformed before our eyes by the timely advent of electric traction, motor vehicles, gas and oil fires, and other notable recent inventions. A few years ago the East End of London was crowded with squalid lodging-houses, in which the people were packed, often so closely that one-third lived in single rooms, one-third in rooms housing two families, and one-third in rooms in which three families or more were herded together. Like conditions prevailed to some extent in all large cities and great towns throughout the kingdom.

The whole of these deplorable conditions are being altered as if by magic. The coming of electric trams and "tubes," carrying the people far out quickly at very small cost; the reducing of fares by railways, 'buses, taxicabs and motor vehicles; the general speeding-up and cheapening of traffic – all these things are combining to make it possible for working and middle class people in large numbers to live out in pretty garden suburbs. Meanwhile gas and oil engines and electric motors are superseding steam engines in town factories. Gas fires are becoming general for cooking and warmth in houses. These things are relieving the air of the town from smoke and smuts. It will soon be possible to grow roses again in the heart of London, and we shall have even our manufacturing towns possessing some of the pleasant features of garden cities. In the rural districts the labourers are acquiring allotments, and the cottagers showing new pride in their gardens. There never was so hopeful a time for the dear old country.

Edwd. Owen Greening

❧ Small Gardens ❧

By T. W. Sanders,
(President of the National Amateur Gardeners' Association.)

A small garden may be roughly estimated to include backyards, designated by the immortal author of "Pickwick" as "enclosed bits of dirt"; those narrow strips, ten feet in width and twenty to thirty feet in length, enclosed with open palings, and frequently seen in a congested area like the East End of London. It also includes those slightly larger and more respectable looking plots attached to the average villa in the suburbs. And besides these, those still larger gardens of a quarter of an acre or so which exist on the outskirts of suburbs, and are somewhat palatial as compared with the preceding ones.

❧ Backyard Gardens ❧

A backyard! Is it really possible to make these unlovely spots beautiful? This is a question very frequently put to the writer in his editorial capacity. We say that it is quite practicable to ensure a beautiful garden in ninety-nine cases out of every hundred, providing the task is performed in the right way. It is really astonishing what may be done at a little cost, and with a little taste and labour, in the way of beautifying dreary spots. Instead of a narrow border, with pieces of rotten board for an edging, procure some burrs, clinkers, or flints, and form a border, with an irregular outline, all round the yard. Let this border vary in width from one to four or five feet, and, if it terminate in a shady corner, form there a rockery. In the centre form one or two roundish or oval beds, with outlines of burrs, flints, or broken bricks, and then you have the groundwork of a pretty garden [see Plan I opposite]. Dig the soil two or three spits deep, work in plenty of horse manure, also ashes, if the soil be clayey. If at all sour, dig in lime, using a spadeful to a square yard. When the ground is dug, plant creepers to cover the side and end walls. The Virginian creeper (*Ampelopsis hederacea*) and Raegner's ivy are good kinds for a shady north or east wall; and *Clematis Jackmanii, Jasminum nudiflorum*, and variegated ivies, for sunny west and south walls. Plant these between October and March. Do not attempt to grow roses; they require more air and sunshine than is possible in a backyard.

If you have room for a shrub or two, plant *Aucuba japonica* or *Euonymus japonica* as evergreens; and the Mock Orange *(Philadelphus coronarius)* or Flowering Currant (*Ribes sanguineum*) as deciduous ones. In the sunny borders plant in autumn or spring such hardy perennials as the Golden Rod (*Solidago virgaurea*), early flowering Chrysanthemums, *Tradescantia virginiana, Lilium candidum, Lilium tigrinum,* Goat's Rue *(Galega officinalis)*, London Pride, and Creeping Jenny. In the shady borders, Lily of the Valley, Solomon's Seal, *Saxifraga cordifolia purpurea*, hardy British ferns, Periwinkle, London Pride, Creeping Jenny, and Stonecrop will grow. The list is a short one, but it is always better to grow a few kinds in large quantities really well than a dozen that only eke out a miserable existence. In April sow some of the excellent One & All hardy annual seeds in vacant spaces, and plant out a few Zonal Pelargoniums, Petunias, Ten-Week Stocks, African Marigolds, and Lobelia in sunny spots, and Calceolarias, French Pansies, Musk, and Monkey Flowers in the shady ones. If space permits, Dahlias may be planted, but these require plenty of sun. When autumn arrives, plant bulbs, especially Crocus, Tulips, Hyacinths, Daffodils, Scillas, and Snowdrops. Seeds of annual climbers, like the Japanese Hop and the Canary Creeper, may be sown at the foot of a shady wall or fence, and those of the common or tall Nasturtium and the tall Convolvulus at the base of sunny walls. These creepers will quickly cover a large space, and add to the beauty of the garden.

There are other ways of making the backyard attractive. A dustbin, for example, may be partly screened from view by a piece of expanding trellis, painted green. A few seeds of Nasturtium, Canary Creeper, or Japanese Hop, sown at the base in April, will result eventually in a complete living screen of foliage and flowers, and look remarkably pretty. A dry, ugly corner may be beautified by placing a heap of mould therein, dropping a few pieces of broken flint or burr on

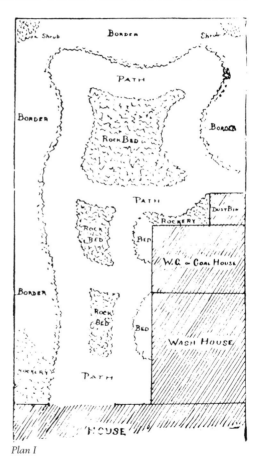

Plan I

19

AFRICAN MARIGOLD

the surface to form tiny beds, and planting these with Stonecrop, Houseleek, and London Pride. A shady, moist corner can be similarly treated, planting Ferns and Creeping Jenny in addition to the other plants. The space between the beds may be composed of cinders, gravel, ballast, concrete, or asphalt, according to taste and means. Above all things, avoid the hideous practice of whitewashing flints, using coloured glass, or dotting oyster and other white shells about; they look common, hideous, and Cockneyfied, and should never be seen in *a garden of taste*. Arrange or plant everything naturally; avoid straight lines and rows of plants; plant in groups or masses; and have the outlines of the beds as irregular as possible. Tolerate no bare walls; plant perennial or evergreen Creepers; and try in every way to make the wall look green, if nothing more.

⋙ Small Villa Gardens ⋘

But we must hark away to the larger type of gardens or we shall not be able to carry out our programme fully [see Plan II overleaf]. These, we will assume, are not hedged in with lofty

Dahlias

buildings, obscuring the light, shutting out sunshine, and preventing the access of fresh air, but are fairly open; such gardens as these will grow a greater variety of plants, and be productive of greater interest to their owners, than a backyard, however well managed and tended.

Here also straight walks and borders with board edgings should be avoided. Burrs, broken bricks, flints, or clinkers should be employed for edgings, and the borders and beds should have irregular outlines. The

The Editor's charming back garden in Lewisham, c. 1905

side fences, if open, may be utilised for growing Scarlet-runner Beans in summer. These will look pretty when in bloom, while their pods will be useful for cooking later on. The borders can be planted with hardy perennials like the perennial Sunflower, Larkspur, Lupin, Lilies of sorts, Pæonies, Chrysanthemums, Sweet Williams, Carnations, and Violas on the sunny sides; and perennial Phloxes, *Anemone japonica*, Michaelmas Daisies, Golden Rod, *Lilium auratum*, Solomon's Seal, Lilies of the Valley, Pansies, London Pride, Creeping Jenny, Stonecrop, and Auriculas on the shady ones. In April hardy annuals, such as Sunflowers, Cornflowers,

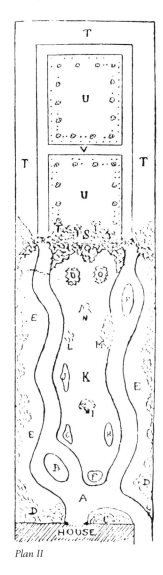

Plan II

annual Chysanthemums, Mignonette, Coreopsis, Candytuft, and Lupins may be sown in patches in the sunny parts; and Virginian Stock, Dwarf Nasturtiums, Love-in-a-Mist, Prince's Feather, and the common Balsam (*Impatiens glandulifera*) in the shady spots.

The beds, if any, can be planted with seedling African Marigolds, Ten-Week Stocks, China Asters, Zinnias, *Phlox Drummondi* or Indian Pinks, or with Zonal Pelargoniums, Fuchsias, Marguerites, and the like. Bulbs can of course be planted in autumn, and if desired, a few evergreens or deciduous shrubs. Supposing that Runner Beans are not cared for, sow good patches of tall Nasturtiums, Canary Creeper, Japanese Hop, tall Convolvulus, and Sweet Peas, and let these run up the fence. The house walls, if shady, can be planted with Virginian Creeper and Raegner's Ivy; the sunny ones with *Ampelopsis Veitchii* and *Clematis Jackmanii*. Ugly corners can be beautified by means of a rockery planted with hardy ferns, Periwinkle, London Pride, and Creeping Jenny, if shady; and a few shrubs and flowers if sunny. Window sills, too, may be made attractive in the same way and with similar materials to those described in connection with the backyard garden.

⤷ Moderate Villa Gardens ⤶

And now we come to the larger garden, surrounded by walls or fences, fairly well exposed, and providing room for the growth of flowers and a few vegetables [see Plan III]. Here there is abundant scope for anyone to make the most of their resources, and ensure not only a pretty but a profitable and useful garden. As a general rule, the boundary walls or fences are not utilised profitably. In many instances they are bare and unfurnished with creepers or fruit trees; in others the climbers are unsuitable, and therefore useless, and hence valuable space is wasted. Most of these boundary walls or fences do not exceed five feet in height. To plant espalier or fan-trained fruit-trees against these is sheer folly and crass stupidity, since in a year or so after planting the trees

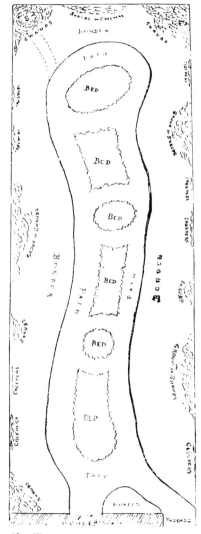

Plan III

reach the top of the wall, or fence, and if close pruning is resorted to in order to keep them within due bounds, they invariably make rank growth, become unfruitful, and a rendezvous for insect pests of all kinds. Away with such trees, then; they only encumber the ground. If fruit-trees are required, plant the cordon form of tree, which has one stem and fruit spurs along its entire length. These, planted at an angle of 45 degrees, and 18 inches apart, will not outgrow their limits, will bear freely, be easy to manage, and in every way better for the purpose. Apples, Pears, Plums, Cherries, Gooseberries, and Currants can be obtained trained in this way from 1s. to 1s. 6d. each. Pears do best on a south aspect; Apples, Plums, and Cherries on an east and west aspect; and Gooseberries and Currants on a north aspect. If fruit is not required, then plant the south wall or fence with Tea and Noisette Roses; the north ones with the Fire-thorn (*Cratægus pyracantha*), a beautiful berry-bearing shrub; *Cotoneaster microphylla*, another berried evergreen; the Boursault, and the evergreen Roses and *Clematis vitalba*; the east with variegated ivies, Japanese Quince (*Cydonia japonica*), and *Clematis Jackmanii*; the west with *Jasminum nudiflorum*, the Gold-netted Honeysuckle (*Lonicera brachypoda aurea-reticulata* – a remarkably long name, by the way, for so simple and pretty a plant), the fragrant winter-flowering *Chimonanthus fragrans*, *Berberis stenophylla*, and some of the Clematis. These would afford a great variety of colour, and be of interest in all seasons.

❧ Shady Gardens ❧

By T. W. Sanders, F.R.H.S., F.L.S., &c.

I T is a common, but nevertheless a mistaken, notion that a perfect and a beautiful garden can only be obtained where the genial rays of bright and glorious sunshine are able to flood every nook and corner with brilliant light and genial warmth.

I fancy I hear many hundreds of readers of these popular garden books say, "We have tried over and over again to make our sunless gardens bright and interesting, but have failed to succeed, and so we feel sure it must be true that it is impossible to have a really pretty and interesting garden where there is little, if any, sunshine to make the flowers grow." But, gentle reader, because you have failed

to succeed in solving the problem, how to secure a charming floral paradise in the absence of sunshine, yet it by no means follows that it cannot be done by those who go the right way about the task. There are beautiful gardens of shade as well as beautiful gardens of light, and happy indeed is the enthusiastic amateur gardener who has his garden half in light and half in shade. The two combined form a delightfully pleasing contrast to each other when properly cultivated.

✤ What to Avoid ✤

Why so many fail to attain success in the creation and management of a pretty shady garden is because they attempt to do impossible things. For instance, they aim at making a shady nook or corner as bright and effective in colouring as is possible in sunny ones. They ignore the well-known practical fact that flowering plants, as a rule, require an abundance of that indispensable element sunshine to enable them to develop their blossoms to the highest perfection, and straightway plant them in sunless positions where they rarely do more than produce foliage. The result of this experiment is, of course, disappointment, and the conception of a false idea that it is useless planting anything attractive in shady spots. Now, there are flowers, and a still larger number of other plants, that delight in shade, and which would, if properly selected and judiciously planted, succeed with the greatest success, and be in every way as interesting and as beautiful as those planted under the genial influence of sunshine. The great secret of the whole thing is to know what kinds will thrive in shade and otherwise. We have only to turn to Nature to discover the truth of the foregoing facts. In the woodland, the gorge, the dell, or the ravine we find some of the most charming and beautiful floral scenes that it is possible to behold.

❧ Shady Borders ❧

There is a shady border in every garden. The south end of a garden faces the north, and consequently gets no sun, and it frequently happens that borders facing north-east or north-west get very little sunshine also. Then, again, there are sometimes borders facing the south, east, and west that are so overshadowed by trees or walls, or lofty buildings as to be more or less sunless. No matter what the aspect may be, if the border or borders fail to get sunshine, they come within the definition of shady borders, and should be planted accordingly. In small gardens there is little scope for tree and shrub planting, hence flowering and foliage plants must therefore be relied upon to furnish the borders. But in gardens of ample extent trees and shrubs form a most desirable background to smaller plants, and therefore ought always to be planted largely. These being of larger growth can obtain a fair amount of sunshine, but not so the more lowly, hardy plants. I shall not, therefore, deal with trees or shrubs in detail; only with flowering and foliage plants. The plants should not be disposed in such a way that all the tall ones are planted at the back, the next size in front, and so on; but so placed that their heights are broken up to form a series of hills and dales, so to speak. For example, one group of tall plants may be at the back, another half-way across, and yet another well out to the front. There should be no regular or systematic arrangement either in the size or position of the groups of plants.

❧ The Plants for such a Border ❧

May consist of the Giant Knotweed (*Polygonum cuspidatum or sachalinense)*; the Martagon Lily (*Lilium Martagon)*; Hanson's Lily (*Lilium Hansonii*); Japanese Lily (*Lilium speciosum*), white and red;

Lilies in pots in a town garden, c. 1910

Goat's Beard Spiræa (*Spiræa aruncus*); Monk's Hood (*Aconitum japonicum* or *Napellus*); Perennial Larkspurs (*Delphiniums*); Foxgloves; Day Lily (*Hemerooallis fulva*); Golden Rod (*Solidago canadense*); Yellow Loose Strife (*Lysimachia thyrsiflora*) ; and the Purple Loose Strife (*Lythrum purpureum*). The foregoing vary in height from three to five feet. Those averaging one to three feet are Columbines (*Aquilegias*); German Irises in variety; Japanese Anemones (Anemone japonica); Leopard's Bane (*Doronicum Plantagineum* and *Clusii*); Spiderwort (*Tradescantia Virginica*); *Campanula persicifolia* and *macrantha*; *Iris graminea*; Gardener's Garter Grass (*Phalangium varie gatum*); and Hardy Ferns, such as the Male, Hardy, Ostrich, and Royal kinds. Of smaller plants the London Pride, Creeping Jenny, Variegated Plantain Lily (*Funkia, Sieboldi variegata*), Coloured Primroses, Christmas Roses, Lilies-of-the-valley, White Rock Cress (Arabis albida), *Saxifraga cœspitosa* and *hypnoides*, and Campanula carpatica. Between these the following bulbs will also do well:– *Scilla campanulata*, white, rose, and blue; Snow-drops; Crocuses; American Cowslip (*Dodecatheon Meadia*); Snowflakes (*Leucojum Æestivum*); and Daffodils. In summer, vacant spaces may be filled with Fuchsias, Calceolarias, and Mimulus; or seeds of Love-lies-bleeding, and Nasturtiums.

To get the very best effect, I recommend the foregoing plants to be planted in bold groups of three, six, or a dozen. By so doing, a good display is obtained the first season. Another advantage to be gained by this system of grouping several plants together is, it affords a good opportunity of bringing bold groups to the front, and so forming bays in which the dwarfer plants may be placed. Where the borders are five or six feet wide, I advise a bush or two of the Japanese Rose (*Rosa rugosa*), the Variegated Euonymus (*Euonymus japonicus variegatus*), the Silver-leaved Maple (*Acenegundo*), or the Purpler leaved Plum (*Prunus Pissardii*), to be planted.

CARTER'S "VICTORIA" PRIZE CALCEOLARIAS

✣ Shady Corners ✣

There are few gardeners that do not possess sunless corners which are more or less unsatisfactory, so far as floral attractiveness is concerned. The ordinary kinds of flowers have been tried, and these having failed to succeed, it is assumed that it is useless planting anything except laurels or some other shrub; indeed, more often than not the corner is utilised as a rubbish heap, and if within the general view of the garden, forms a most unsightly object. Now there is really no legitimate excuse for the existence of these ugly spots. They may be made just as attractive and just as pretty and interesting as the sunny positions. By the exercise of a little taste and skill, a rockery may be formed of burrs or large stones, or even of large tree trunks and branches, and good mould, and then planted with an assortment of ferns and other plants which I shall presently name. The burrs or stones must not be arranged too formally; that is to say, the surface must not be made to assume an even appearance, but made so as to appear as rugged and diversified in outline as possible. On no account use white plates, fish shells, fused glass, or clinkers. These materials are too cocknified, and too utterly out of character with the beautiful foliage of the plants to form a pretty and attractive rockery. The larger and more rugged the burrs or stones, the more pleasing will the rockery be. Arrange them so as to form a series of beds, varying from two or three feet to a foot in width. Before starting to place the burrs or stones, see that a good foundation is laid. The lower strata may consist of broken bricks, small stones, and rubbish generally. On this, place a layer of decayed vegetable matter and rough mould, then finish off with a foot or so of the best mould you can get. Now fix the burrs or stones, half burying some, and partially so others, while a few may simply rest on the surface. You will now have a series of beds in which it will be necessary to place a few inches of good compost – equal parts of loam, leaf-mould, and sand. If choice ferns are to be grown, a little peat will also be needful.

❧ Plants for a Shady Rockery ❧

Where expense is a primary consideration, the rockery may be planted with Solomon's Seal, Male Fern (*Lastrea filix-mas*), Lady Fern (*Athyrium filix-fœmina*), Buckler Fern (*Lastrea rigida*), Prickly-Toothed Fern (*Lastrea spinulosa*), Royal Fern (*Osmunda regalis*), Shield Fern (*Polystichum angulare*), Hart's Tongue Fern (*Scolopendrium vulgare*), Hard Fern (*Blechnum spicant*), London Pride (*Saxifraga umbrosa*), Golden and Common Creeping Jenny, Dwarf Spindle Bush (*Euonymus radicans variegata*), Rock Foils (*Saxifraga cœspitosa* and *hypnoides*), and Sedums in variety. These plants will make a most pleasing effect from spring till late in autumn, and often eclipse in quiet beauty and grace the more favoured parts of the garden. Where expense is no object, such a rockery may be planted solely with choice ferns, to wit, American Maidenhair Fern (*Adiantum pedatum*), Black Spleenwort (*Asplenium adiantum nigrum*); Green Spleenwort (*Asplenium viride*), Sensitive Fern (Onoclea sensibilis), Ostrich Fern (*Struthiopteris Germanica*), Cinnamon Fern (*Osmunda cinnamomea*). Polypody Ferns (*Polypodium Cambricum, dryopteris* and *vulgare)*, Bladder Ferns (*Cystopteris fragilis* and *montana*). These, with the commoner kinds previously given, will form the basis of a really attractive fern rockery. Others may be added from time to time if desired. Here and there bulbs of *Scilla*

campanulata, Snowdrops and Crocuses, and corms and tubers of *Cyclamen œderhfolium* and *europœum*, and Winter Aconites, may be planted to give a cheery appearance to the rockery in early spring.

❧ Grottoes ❦

In some gardens there are corners partly hidden from view by groups of shrubs, and overshadowed by trees, that might be turned to pleasing account by forming grottoes of artificial rockwork, and planting them with ferns and other shade-loving plants. This artificial rockwork may be constructed with rough burrs, fixed by means of cement, and afterwards coated with a mixture of cement and red sand. The burrs may have to be secured in the desired position by means of stout wire or iron rods. The whole should be arranged in as natural and picturesque a manner as possible. If there be a fairly good water supply, a series of cascades may be formed down the face of the grotto, with a shallow pond at the base. The water may be supplied through a pipe furnished with a stop-cock, so that it can be turned off or on at will. In the pond or basin, fish may be allowed to disport themselves. The rockwork may be clothed with Ivies, Creeping Jenny, Mother-o'-Thousands, Royal and Marsh Ferns, Maidenhair, Spleenworts, etc., and so made exceedingly interesting and pretty.

The Snowdrop, or Galanthus nivalis

A Foreword by the Editor

IS it entirely national egotism which makes an Englishman feel as he walks through the gardens of sunnier lands that there is something more tenderly beautiful in those at home? No. There is one chief feature of pleasure gardens which more nearly approaches perfection in these islands of ours than else where, and which gives to all other garden features an added charm. It is the exquisite beauty of our grass lawns. The delight with which they inspire us is not felt by Englishmen alone. Every foreign visitor feels it also, and frankly confesses that, in this respect, British supremacy is beyond question. Wonderful stories are told of costly efforts made by American millionaires and Continental noblemen to reproduce near their own homes similar lawns of rich emerald green, soft, smooth, and velvet-like as ours. In vain are their ingenious devices of artificial sprayings. We can afford to rest secure in the certainty that the superiority of our lawns will ever remain unchallenged and unchallengeable until some syndicate can be formed rich and powerful enough to buy up and divert the Gulf Stream, which surrounds our islands with genially warm seas, and endows them with the sweet, soft, moist air we enjoy.

Fine-leaved Sheep's Fescue, or Festuca ovina tenuifolia

Lawns

By W. J. Stevens, F.R.H.S

Lawn Management

THE first essential is a good foundation, effectually drained, either naturally or artificially. The lawn must rest upon a base which will permit of no sinkages. The surface of a lawn may follow any form which suits the natural conformation of the ground. It may be level, as a bowling-green, or run up steep slopes and over rounded hills; or dip down into valleys and glades or circle round masses of shrubs; but the surface must ever be level and smooth. There must be no erratic excrescences; no holes or meaningless depressions; no hollows caused by subsidence due to defects in the foundation or to unequal depth of made earth or other circumstances. The effect of a lawn is ruined by accidental irregularities. It is the carpet of the garden. Any break in its smoothness is a detriment. And this maxim is true of evenness of colour and elasticity, as well as of surface. The base upon which the soil of the lawn rests must, therefore, be of a character which will not permit water to stagnate about the roots of the grasses, nor allow moisture to dry quickly out of the soil after a few hours of dry weather. It is not of little importance to press this upon attention. If the foundation be good, the next point is the soil. Inexperienced lawn-makers often use all sorts of varying ground materials which are conveniently to hand, and the soil underlying the grass varies accordingly from richly manured earth and clay soil to barren sand. The result is patchiness of the grass, disappointing and puzzling to the novice. The soil should be good in heart, but not overstocked with manure. If poor, it should be enriched with leaf mould or a moderate quantity of thoroughly decomposed dung. Where it is of good quality no additional fertility need be dug in, but it should be evenly trenched to a depth of half a yard, or even more, and it is essential that the depth of worked soil should be equal throughout. If the natural soil is shallow, it should be made at least a foot deep by adding good soil.

◈ Lawn Making with Turf ◈

A lawn can be more quickly created by using turf, but it is not easy to procure it of fine quality, free from docks, daisies, and coarse grasses. The owner of a spreading expanse of fine, clean grass turf is not usually inclined to cut it up in strips for lawn-making. The turf that is obtainable is more frequently full of weeds. In importing it into our gardens we bring in trouble. However, where suitable turf is available, it is commonly cut into strips a yard long and a foot wide. It should be about 1½ inches in thickness, and be carefully rolled up and brought direct from its old bed to its new quarters. It should be laid as soon as possible after cutting. If there is an interval of frost between the cutting of the turves and relaying of them, the rolls should be protected from being frozen. To assist the grasses to root in their new bed, the surface of the soil should

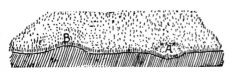

be lightly dug over to a depth of two or three inches, assuming it to have settled down close and solid. The laying of the turves will then be a question of workman-like care. The joints must be made close, and

A Lawn Imperfectly Made. A is a hollow, B a hump. The hollow must be raised and the hump brought down before the lawn is satisfactorily laid.

as each turf is laid it should be lightly beaten down, reserving a more energetic beating until the whole is laid. In finishing off the lawn the turf-beater should be well applied until a level surface is produced and the joints of the turf are closed. A heavy roller should finally be passed over the lawn, and a period of rest from disturbance should follow until the roots have taken a fresh hold and new growth is evident.

Lawn Making with Seeds

The general preference we express for making a lawn anew from seed is based on good reason. During the past quarter of a century the growing of fine grasses for seed has been developed in Germany until it has become, like the bulb growing in Holland, a business upon which whole districts of people are supported. The grasses are grown by peasant cultivators, who own their small areas of land and religiously preserve each field for one kind of grass from year to year, and generation to generation. Sometimes whole villages will unite to ensure that only one kind of fine grass is grown in the district and no admixture admitted. By this means, by systematic cleaning of the land from weeds, and by the admirable system of constant testing made possible by Government establishing local stations for the purpose, a remarkable degree of purity in grass seeds has been arrived at. A British seed-merchant can obtain exactly what he desires through the great Continental collectors, who buy from the peasants. He can have almost perfection of purity guaranteed if he is wise enough to be willing to pay for it. And if his establishment possesses the most modern machinery, he can raise the standard of germination by eliminating all light and dead seeds, all chaff and dirt, and such weeds as may perchance remain in the bulk, notwithstanding the care of the German cultivators.

Before sowing the seed the soil should be lightly and evenly raked over. The seed should be sown quite evenly over the entire surface. To enable the sower to do this, let him choose a fine, calm day for the work. When the seeds are sown, they should be raked well in, or sifted soil should be scattered lightly over. The sowing being complete, a roller should be passed over the surface. Nothing then remains to be done for the present but to string cotton threads over the newly sown seeds, or protect them with fine-meshed tanned netting from the too solicitous attentions of the birds. When it is observed that a good covering of young grass clothes the surface, the tops should be shaved off with a scythe.

◈ After Management ◈

On no account must the lawn-mowing machine be used at first. The young shoots have not strength enough in their early days to bear the lifting and disturbing action of machine-cutting. Rolling should follow the scythe work to spread out the roots and consolidate the lawn surface. The subsequent treatment is a matter of constant rolling and cutting – cutting and rolling. The cutting stimulates the roots below to tiller. In the first two or three summers of the infancy of a lawn close cutting of the grass should be avoided. The knives of a modern machine are easily adjusted. Let them be set high for the sake of the tender grasses until even the finest species are thoroughly established. Close cutting in summer bares the roots to

Shows how the surface may be saved from injury by the shoes in working. A board is tied over the shoe.

38

A family relaxes by their conservatory, c. 1910

the intense heat of direct sun-rays, and in autumn leaves them open to the attacks of early frosts. In dry weather it is a good plan to forego the use of the grass-box in front of the machine. The young lawn in its first years must be watched for the appearance of dandelions, plantains, and daisies. As soon as these show, they must be uprooted, or they will quickly spread. "Ill weeds grow apace," and especially flourish on the carefully prepared surface of a well-made English lawn.

❧ Window Gardens ❦

By T. W. Sanders, F.R.H.S.

THERE is no phase of gardening more delightful and captivating than that of cultivating flowers in the immediate surroundings of the home – on the window-sill, the balcony, the porch, and in the dwelling-rooms. It yields infinite pleasure to those who, having no garden or greenhouse, have no other means of cultivating the choicest and noblest of God's gifts – flowers of all climes. As a rule, plants grown thus are tended with more love and care than those grown in other ways. They are regarded as children needing the utmost care and watchfulness to enable them to develop their highest and noblest characteristics. And no wonder, seeing

the important part even the simplest of flowers play in imparting brightness, happiness, and pleasure to the home and those who dwell within it. Without flowers no house can be said to be bright or cheerful. In the dullest and dreariest parts of our crowded cities we often see noble attempts being made to impart a little sunshine and pleasure into the lives and houses of the dwellers by the cultivation of the Creeping Jenny, the Virginian Creeper, Ivy, or some other even more attractive plant. Every horticultural society throughout the kingdom ought to foster the culture of window plants in every possible way. Prizes should be offered for the best examples of plants grown indoors, as well as for the best decorated window-sills. Many societies do this already, but they do not represent a tithe of those which might and could do it if they chose.

Window Boxes

We will begin with plants in boxes. The first thing to claim our attention is the question of the best form of box to use. There are many forms of boxes in use. Some are made of plain wood, others of wood ornamented in front with virgin cork, split hazel, and larch wood; and others, again, exhibit the taste, skill, and ingenuity of their owners in fancy woodwork or in metals,

Fig 1.– Plain window box ornamented with virgin cork.

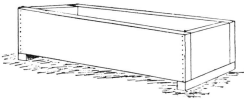

Fig 2.– Construction of plain window box.

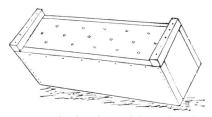

Fig 3.– *Window box showing holes made in the bottom for drainage.*

Fig 4.– *Window box decorated with strips of hazel wood.*

ornamented with glazed tiles or other pretty designs. As a guide to those who desire to make their own boxes, we give a few designs of useful and pretty types of window-boxes. *Fig. 1* represents one of the best and most appropriate styles. The box itself is made as described in the next paragraph, and as depicted in our engraving *(Fig. 2)*, and then covered with pieces of virgin cork affixed to the front by means of French nails. The cork may be improved in appearance by giving it a coating of size and then one of varnish, or by the application of a coat of brown or green paint. Another serviceable and artistic box, which anyone skilled in woodwork can easily make, is represented by *(Fig. 4)*. This consists of a framework *(Fig. 2)* with strips of hazel wood, having the natural bark on, arranged in the manner shown in the illustration. The hazel strips are nailed to the box by means of French nails, and afterwards sized and varnished. A box of this kind will last almost a lifetime.

A simpler kind of box is depicted in the illustration *(Fig. 6)*. The framework is made as shown at *Fig. 2*, and the front covered with split pieces of larch having the bark on. This, when sized and varnished, will also prove a durable box. Another form of box which a carpenter or joiner could make in his spare time is first made in the plain style shown in *Fig. 2*, and decorated with ornamental beading. The next style illustrated *(Fig. 5)* is of a more elaborate and costly nature. Boxes of this kind can be purchased ready made of any ironmonger, or made by any skilled worker in metals. The main body of the box (see *Fig. 2*) may be formed of zinc or sheet iron, or, if preferred, of wood. An ornamental beading of iron or wood must be affixed round the edges of the box, and the remaining space filled with glazed ornamental tiles embedded in putty, plaster of Paris, or cement. The pattern

Fig 5.– Window box of wood or iron decorated with glazed tiles.

Fig 6.– Window box simply decorated with split pieces of larch.

of tile shown in the illustration is an original one designed by the artist who made the sketches, but there are plenty of other patterns equally as pretty that would serve the purpose just as well. We would, however, caution the reader against selecting tiles of bright or vivid colours, like scarlet, blue, or yellow. Soft and pleasing shades of green or brown harmonise best with the colours of the flowers.

✣ Plants for Window Gardens ✣

In dealing with the question of plants, we have to consider the various aspects of the windows. For example, some probably never receive any direct sunshine, while others are fully exposed to it. Now, all plants will not succeed alike in sun or shade, and so it is necessary to select those adapted for each. Windows facing north are practically sunless, and here hardy Ferns, Creeping

Jenny, Periwinkle, Calceolarias, Fuchsias, and Musk will do best for summer decoration; while for autumn and winter decoration, shrubs such as Euonymus, Aucubas, Box, and Ivies, are suitable; and for a spring display, Crocuses and Snowdrops. An eastern window gets, of course, the morning sun, and here Fuchsias will do well; so also will Dwarf and Tall Nasturtiums, Sweet-Scented Tobacco, Godetias, and Canary Creepers for summer flowering. In autumn plant the shrubs named for north aspect, also Crocuses, Snowdrops, Daffodils, Forget-me-not, and Auriculas for spring blooming.

In a western aspect Ivy-leaved Pelargoniums, Marguerites, Petunias, Lobelia, and Tropæolum Lobbianum will succeed admirably in summer. In autumn plant hardy shrubs, like the Euonymus, *Cupressus Lawsoniana*, *Thuia Lobbii*, Variegated Ivies, and Aucubas, to keep the boxes gay during the winter. In autumn, also, plant Tulips, Hyacinths, Crocuses, Daffodils, Snowdrops, *Aubretia purpurea*, and Wall-flowers for spring flowering. A south aspect may be planted with similar flowers, bulbs, and shrubs, adding also, Mignonette, Zonal Pelargoniums, Nasturtiums, Heliotropes, and *Gazania splendens*, for summer blooming. If the list we have given is not sufficient, Violas and Pansies may be grown on the east aspect, and Stocks, Asters, Annual Chrysanthemums, and French Marigolds on the west and south aspects. Those who can only afford hardy annuals should sow Dwarf and Tall Nasturtiums in boxes on the east and west aspects, and Mignonette, Godetias, Annual Chrysanthemums, Virginian Stock, Candytuft, and Canary Creeper in those on the other aspects.

Godetia

Gonium, Petunia, and *Tropæolum Lobbianum*, should be planted near the edge of the box in order that their shoots may fall over and hide the front entirely. Tall plants, like Marguerite, etc., should be planted at the back, and dwarf ones midway between these and the drooping plants.

❧ Cultivation ❧

The general cultural details to be observed are few and simple. Always make the soil quite firm at the time of planting. Give a good watering at once to settle the soil, and afterwards see that the latter is never allowed to get dry. Beyond training the shoots of Tall Nasturtiums and Canary Creepers up the sides of the window as they grow, we do not think there is any important detail that we have over-looked in the management of window-boxes.

A lady waters her window box

❧ Indoor Gardens ❧

By T. W. Sanders, F.L.S., F.R.H.S.

❧ Care and Management of Plants in Rooms ❧

INDOOR gardening is undoubtedly a subject which commends itself to every flower lover, since it is a hobby which may be pursued with equal success by rich and poor, weak and strong. The invalid who is confined to the house, and unable to participate in the pleasures of outdoor gardening, or even to grow flowers on a window sill, is able to cultivate at least a few plants in the dwelling-room under congenial conditions, while the pleasure derived from so fascinating a pursuit is immeasurable. The writer, in his capacity of Editor of a journal which caters for Amateur Gardeners, has often been deeply touched by the letters of invalids in which the writers have described the unspeakable joy they have experienced in cultivating such simple plants as Musk, Creeping Jenny, and Ivy in their rooms. It is very evident, therefore, that indoor gardening does confer a great amount of pleasure upon those who are so unfortunate as not to enjoy such good health as will permit them to take part in outdoor gardening. To those who enjoy that greatest of all earthly blessings – good health – and are able to cultivate flowers outdoors as well as indoors, the pleasure is of a two-fold nature.

Plants add greatly to the attractiveness and cheerfulness of a room, especially in the case of a cottager's or artisan's home, which would oftentimes be dull if it were not for the presence of a few bright flowers in the window. Even in well-appointed rooms a few plants placed about make them decidedly more cheerful, if not attractive. And so, on the whole, it may truly be said that indoor plant culture yields infinite pleasure to those who practice the art, and at the same time adds to the attractiveness of the home.

There are several ways in which indoor gardening may be practised. For example, flowering plants like the Fuchsia, Musk, or Geranium may be grown on the inner ledge of a window; Ferns, etc., cultivated in Wardian cases or under a bell-glass; foliage plants like Palms and India-rubber Plants grown in ornamental pots about the room, and so on.

In small rooms, especially those occupied by the cottager or artisan, the first plan is the one in general vogue. This not only renders the room bright and cheerful from the inside, but also attractive from the outside, and may therefore be regarded as a suitable plan to adopt by those who like to make their windows attractive to passers-by. Indeed, where flowering plants are preferred to those with ornamental foliage, the former must be grown thus on account of the sunlight required to develop and perfect the blossoms. Fern cases should also be placed not too far from the light, although they should not be exposed to direct sunlight. Foliage plants and Ferns will do almost anywhere in a room; Palms doing as well as

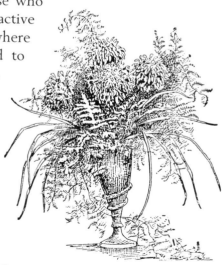

A vase of chrysanthemums

47

CARTERS BRILLIANT PRIZE CINERARIAS

any in the darkest positions. It should, however, be borne in mind as a general rule that all plants like exposure to light, and therefore should, wherever possible, be placed in a light position.

Supposing, then, that some of the readers of these pages wish to grow plants so as to make the interior of their windows gay and cheerful, the most important point to decide is what to grow. First of all let us say that there are very few flowering plants that will bloom in sunless rooms. The exceptions are the Fuchsia, Musk, Sweet Scented Tobacco, *Campanula isophylla alba* and Calceolaria. Foliage plants will, however, do well, and the best of these for the purpose are *Aspidistra lurida variegata* India-rubber Plant, *Fatsia japonica*, and *Anthericum variegatum* with the following Ferns: *Pteris serrulata*, *Pteris tremula*, *Asplenium bulbiferum*, *Cyrtomium falcatum*, *Scolopendrium vulgare*, and *Phlebodium aureum*. For growing in suspended baskets or pots close to the window, Saxifraga sarmentosa, Linaria Cymbalaria and Creeping Jenny are excellent plants.

Where windows get a fair amount of sunshine flowering plants will do well. Here is a list from which the reader may make a selection to suit his space and pocket. For summer flowering

Fuchsias, Zonal and Ivy-leaved Geraniums, Petunias, Heliotropes, Hydrangeas, *Lilium auratum, speciosum* and *Harrisii*, Balsams, Cacti, *Vallota purpurea* (Scarboro' Lily), *Agapanthus umbellatus* – Blue African Lily – Oleander, and Marguerites. For autumn flowering: Guernsey Lily (*Nerine sarniensis*) and Early Chrysanthemums. For winter blooming: Chinese Primulas, Cyclamens, and Christmas Roses. For spring flowering: Hyacinths, Tulips, Daffodils, Crocuses, Iris reticulata, Snowdrops, *Spiræa japonica, Azalea indica*, Calla Lilies, Camellias, Cinerarias, and Auriculas. With these may be grown all the year round the Sweet Scented Verbena (*Aloysia citriodora*), Oak-leaf, Peppermint, and Nutmeg Scented Geraniums; while for suspending in the window, the plants recommended for a shady window are *Sedum Sieboldi variegata*, Indian Strawberry (*Fragaria indica*), *Othonna crassifolia, Tradescantia discolor* and *zebrina, Isolepis gracilis*, and the Bermuda Buttercup (*Oxalis cernua*).

The ferns, palms, and foliage plants will require to be watered freely during the spring and summer, and moderately in autumn and winter. In the summer time they may be stood outdoors during a gentle shower to wash off the dust from their leaves, but at other periods the leaves must be sponged with soapy water occasionally.

An elegant flower stand for a hall

Re-potting will not be required every year, but, when necessary do it in March or April.

We will next deal with ornamental leaved and other plants grown in ordinary pots and stood in fancy receptacles about the room. Those in general use for this purpose are the India-rubber Plant (*Ficus elastica*); Parlour Palm (*Aspidistra lurida variegata*) Fig-leaf Palm (*Fatsia Japonica*), frequently called the "Castor Oil Plant," and "Aralia"; ordinary Palms, as *Kentia Belmoreana, Areca lutescens, Phœnix dactylifera* (Date Palm), and rupicola; *Latania Borbonica, Areca sapida, Cocos Weddelliana* and *Corypha australis Grevillea robusta*; Blue Gum Tree (*Eucalyptus globosa*); Elephant's Ear Begonia (*Begonia Rex*); *Dracæna indivisa; Araucaria excelsa Dracæna Bruantii*; Japanese Hyacinth (*Ophiopogon jaburan variegatum*); Club Grass (*Isolepis gracilis*); and ferns, as *Pteris tremula, Pteris serrulata, Nephrodium molle, Adiantum cuneatum Asplenium bulbiferum*, and *Phlebodium aureum*. All these are remarkable for their handsome foliage, and the greater portion of them may be grown for many years in rooms in which gas is not consumed regularly. Where gas is used daily the Aspidistra, Fig-leaf Palm, and *Kentia Belmoreana* are the only plants that can be relied upon to succeed regularly in rooms. Those, however, who have a greenhouse, and can change the plants every three days may grow any of the foregoing which I have mentioned, with fair success. Flowering plants may only be grown in the room when in flower; at other times they must be grown close to a window or in a greenhouse.

We have now to deal with Ferns in Wardian cases, and under bell glasses. This is a delightful phase of indoor gardening. Cases can be purchased ready made through the medium of the Agricultural and Horticultural Association; or they may be constructed by anyone

Wardian case for ferns

skilled in joinery. They are made in all sorts of shapes – plain and ornamental. They are usually fitted with a zinc tray at the bottom, a hole connected with a small pipe fitted with a tap being made at one corner to carry off superfluous moisture. On this tray a layer of stones or crocks has to be placed to serve as drainage. Some moss should overlie this, and then some four to six inches of compost be put on the top. To relieve the flatness of the surface pieces of tufa or sandstone rock should be embedded in the soil to form a miniature rockery and little beds or ledges for the ferns. Smaller cases, consisting of an earthenware base forming a kind of pan, with a rim to receive a glass globe, or shade, are also employed for the same purpose, and the pan is drained and filled with soil and compost in the same way as advised for the Wardian cases. In both instances the compost should consist of equal parts of loam, peat, leaf-mould, and charcoal, with a little silver sand or Jadoo fibre.

The Ferns usually grown in such cases are as follows: –

BRITISH: Hart's tongue (*Scolopendrium vulgare* and its numerous kinds); *Polystichum angulare cristatum* (Shield Fern); *Welsh Polypody* (*Polypodium cambricum*); Crested Male Fern (*Lastrea Filix-mas cristata*); Black Spleenwort (*Asplenium Adiantum nigrum*); *Asplenium trichomanes* and the Native Maidenhair (*Adiantum capillusveneris*).

EXOTIC: *Davallia alpina*, *Asplenium fontanum*, *Doodia caudata*, *Blechnum gracile*, *Pteris cretica*, *Davallia bullata*, *Lomaria Alpina*, and *Asplenium fragrans*. With the Ferns are generally grown a few mosses, as *Selaginella Kraussiana*, *denticulata*, amœna, *grandis*, and *Victoria*.

Another way of growing Ferns in a room is worthy of note here, and that is planting tiny kinds in small ornamental, Jars bowls, and other bric-a-brac. Ferns grown thus do not, however, last in good condition very long, mainly owing to the fact that these receptacles contain no provision for the escape of superfluous water. However, they are pretty, and as the Ferns are not expensive it does not signify about the short duration of their lives when grown thus. These little ornaments can be stood about the rooms on tables, mantelpieces, and so on. When a fern becomes sickly, turn it out and put another in its place. When moisture is needed stand the jars, etc., in a bowl of water for a few minutes.

Yet another novel mode of gardening is that of growing acorns in bottles. The acorn is, of course, the seed of the oak. If one of these can be obtained, pierce it through the centre with a stout needle containing thread. Arrange the thread so that the acorn is suspended point downwards midway in a bottle. Add sufficient water to just touch the point of the acorn, and cover the mouth with a paper capsule. Stand the bottle in a warm place; then in due course the acorn will vegetate and put forth roots, which will coil round the interior of the bottle, also a stem which will ascend through the neck and bear foliage. The chestnut and horse-chestnut may also be grown in bottles. The bottles in this case should, however, be wide-mouthed ones, so as to allow the nuts to rest in the neck, and permit the water to rise and just touch their undersides. Trees so raised will grow for a number of years in bottles provided the water is changed sometimes.

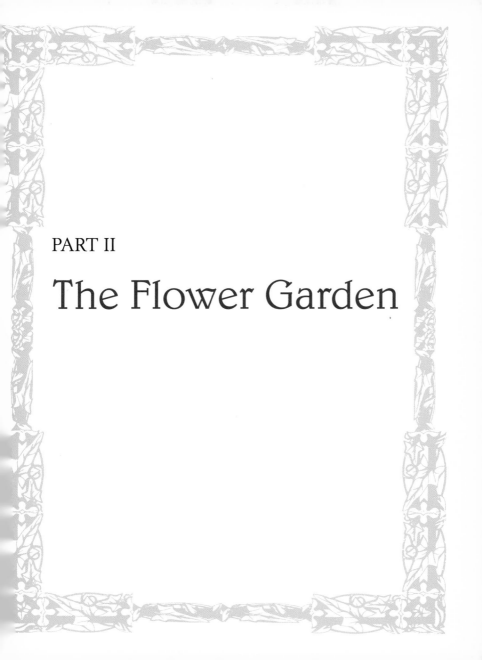

PART II

The Flower Garden

PART II

The Flower Garden

Emerging from the excesses of the Victorian craze for brightly coloured annual bedding plants, gardening in the first decade of the nineteenth century trod a careful line. Hardy perennials, the original backbone of the cottage garden, had for many years been eclipsed by the brash new annuals so easily obtained by seed and so attractively 'cheap and cheerful', but as Mr Sanders pointed out in his booklet No. 5, 'people of taste' were now returning to the culture of 'old fashioned flowers - hardy perennials, bulbs and tubers'. For the economical gardener, unable to afford the actual plants, these could be obtained with a little extra effort and time by raising from seed (a packet of twelve varieties being available from The Agricultural and Horticultural association itself for a mere shilling.). Using as his backbone the most popular of perennials: antirrhinum, phlox, asters, poppies and carnations, the economically challenged gardener envisaged by the 'One & All' writers could mix in the annuals that would provide almost instant colour to his garden. These too could be obligingly provided by 'One & All' as a mixed pack, sized to accommodate large or small gardens. That these annuals were more popular with the readers of the One & All guides despite their morale low-ground, may be indicated by the publication of the booklet on 'Annuals' as No. 2 in the series (after Sweet Peas). Roses a perennial favourite now widely available as standards and hybrids, also merited a specific booklet, whilst some of the more exotic possibilities (the Golden Rayed Japanese Lily for example) were allocated a few tantalising pages in the 1913 'Annual' for those with aspirations beyond the common pansy. Having filled the beds and borders attention was turned to climbers, an essential adjunct to the urban garden confined by high walls and fences, or even the larger garden where division into productive and aesthetic areas was recommended. A series of images in this booklet (No. 14) sought to persuade that however humble the terraced dwelling, however shady the spot, or however poor the tenant, there was a climber for you. Ranging from the delights of the rose or the clematis, to the humbler Canary Creeper or nasturtium, down to the 'beautiful and productive' runner bean covered archway. Even the poorest of soils could raise an ivy to give nobility to an 'East End home'.

Twigs Way

⇌ Perennials ⇋

BY T. W. Sanders, F.L.S., F.R.H.S., &c.

HARDY Perennials are the best of all plants for the adornment of the flower garden. Most of them are of easy culture and possess the excellent merit of longevity; consequently, are just the kind of flowers for those who want to have a beautiful garden of a more or less permanent nature. Once get a garden well stocked with such flowers, there is no necessity to incur a big annual outlay for replenishing the beds and borders, as in the case of hardy annuals and tender plants. Then again, those who

wish to spare no expense in having a beautiful garden, may grow perennials in conjunction with tender flowers and annuals, and so ensure a greater variety of colour and form, as well as a more brilliant display. Time was when hardy perennials formed the only flowers for garden decoration. Then came a change in taste, and these beautiful old flowers, beloved of our grandmothers, were more or less discarded in favour of tender flowers like the geranium, calceolaria, and lobelia. The craze for the latter eventually subsided somewhat, and people of taste, with a love of the really beautiful in plant life, began

Columbine is a hardy alpine perennial. Likes sandy soil with leaf mould. Sow seeds in June, and plant out in October for flowering the following season.

to pay attention to the culture of old-fashioned flowers – hardy perennials, bulbs, and tubers. Year by year more attention is being directed to the cultivation of these plants, and less to the tender ones. This is a step in the right direction, and I hope the day is not far distant when we may see hardy perennials extensively grown in large and small gardens.

It may be of service to the inexperienced amateur gardener if I explain what a hardy perennial really is. It is a plant which lives for an indefinite number of years, and has fibrous roots, as in the campanula; bulbs, as in the case of the lily; or tubers, as in the winter aconite; or corms, as in the case of the cyclamen. It may also be herbaceous or evergreen. If herbaceous, its flower stems and foliage lie down to the soil in the autumn, leaving its roots below, and putting forth new growth in spring. If evergreen, it simply loses its flower stems, but retains a tuft of foliage throughout the year.

❧ Where Perennials may be Grown ❧

Perennials may be grown in town, suburban, or country gardens, but the best results are to be obtained in the suburbs or country, where

Forget-me-not. Hardy perennial. Likes moist situation and good loamy soil. Sow in spring or summer in a warm shady place. Will give a profusion of delicate blue flowers in spring.

Double Sweet William. Hardy biennial. Likes sandy soil with peat. Sow seeds outdoors in light soil in April or May.

the air is pure and there is plenty of light and sunshine. Some sorts do better in the shade, and some best in the sunnier positions of the garden. In the smaller type of gardens, no plants are better adapted for the narrow borders, which constitute the main positions for flower growing than perennials. In gardens of larger extent, they may be grown to excellent advantage in borders, fringing groups of shrubs on lawns, or borders of shrubberies. In such cases the borders must not be narrow, but at least 6 to 10 ft. in width, to enable the plants to be grown to the best possible effect. Perennials may also be grown in large beds on lawns. In very small gardens, the fences at the back of the border may be clothed with the everlasting white and pink peas and double convolvulus. Here and there tall perennial sunflowers, delphiniums, and holly-hocks may come between, and so form a pleasing background to the dwarfer plants.

❧ How to Plant ❧

Fibrous-rooted perennials like the delphinium, lupin, &c., should be planted in groups of three, six, or a dozen plants, according to the width

Mixed carnation marguerite. Hardy perennial, blooms June to September. Sow in February or March in pans of light mould, covering slightly with fine soil. Give ample air and keep soil pleasantly moist.

of the border. This ensures a good bold mass of one colour in a place, and is infinitely more pleasing and effective than planting single specimens. Of course, where the border is only 3 feet wide or less, one plant will suffice. Do not plant in rows, but dispose the tall and dwarf plants so as to form a series of irregular bays. This will prevent the border having a flat appearance, and give it a more diversified and picturesque effect. A bold group of holly-hocks, or of delphiniums, or of lupins, &c., coming out boldly to the front, adds a distinct charm to the border and prevents the

Double Indian Pink. Dwarf hardy biennial. Flowers from May to late summer. Sow seed in sheltered border in September, giving protection against frost in winter. Transplant when ready.

whole of the flowers (in the case of a straight border) being seen at one glance. Then, again, the plants and bulbs should be so arranged that every part of the border is more or less bright and interesting throughout the season.

To make my meaning still clearer, the spring, summer, and autumnal bloomers should be carefully mixed, so that no part of the border is deficient in colour from early spring to late autumn. Thus between the perennials, groups of bulbous plants can be grown to flower in spring. These will have died down ere the perennials have attained sufficient size to require the extra room. In the front of the borders I usually plant groups of snowdrops, crocuses, and scillas, and over these masses of aubrietia, arabis and saxifrage. The bulbs push their way through the green carpet, and flower, and by the time they have ceased to flower and grow, the plants are ready to flower also.

CALENDAR

Of Fibrous-Rooted Perennials

WALLFLOWER. GOLDEN

PRINTED IN SCOTLAND

JANUARY—*Helleborus niger*, white, 1 ft.; *Helleborus colchicus*, rich plum, 1 ft.; *Helleborus Orientalis*, rose, 1 ft.

FEBRUARY—*Anemone blanda*, blue 6 in.; *Helleborus guttatus*, purplish crimson, 1 ft.; *Helleborus olympicus*, white and green, 1 ft.; *Hepatica angulosa*, sky blue, 6 in.; *Hepatica* triloba alba (white), cœrulea (blue), and rubra (red).

MARCH—Primroses, hybrid, various colours, 6 in.; Double Daisies, white and red, 4 in.; Polyanthuses, various colours, 6 in.; *Iberis corifolia*, white, 6 in.; Wallflowers, various, 12 to 18 in.

APRIL—*Adonis vernalis*, yellow, 1 ft.; *Anemone appenina*, blue, 6 in.; *Doronicum Clusii*, yellow, 2 to 3 ft.; *Orobus vernus*, blue, 1 ft.; *Arabis albida*, white, 4 in.; *Aubrietia purpurea*, blue, 3 in.; *Corydalis nobilis*, lilac and yellow, 1 ft.

MAY—*Alyssum saxatile* and *saxatile variegatum*, yellow, 6 in.; *Daphne Cneorum*, pink, 6 in.; *Doronicum plantagineum excelsum*, yellow, 3 ft.; *Erysimum pumilum*, yellow, 6 in.;

Saxifraga Wallaceii, white, 6 in.; *Aubrietia Leichtlinii*, red, 4 in.; *Aubrietia Campbellii*, blue, 4 in.; *Papaver orientale*, crimson, 4 ft.; *Veronica gentianoides*, blue, 18 in. to 2 ft.; *Ranunculus aconitifolius*, fl. pl., white, 18 in.; *Phlox Nelsonii* (white), *procumbens* (lilac), *setacea* (various), 4 in.

CARTERS "HOLBORN" PRIZE PRIMULAS.

JUNE—*Achillea ptarmica*, fl. pl., and "The Pearl," white, 2 to 3 ft.; *Anthericum liliago* and *liliastrum* (white), 18 in.; *Heuchera sanguinea*, red, 18 in.; *Lychnis chalcedonica*, scarlet, 3 ft.; *Lychnis viscaria*, fl. pl., rose, 18. in.; Œnothera speciosa, white, 2 ft.; Œnothera fruticosa, yellow, 2 ft.; Œnothera Youngii, yellow, 18 in.; Columbines (Aquilegias), various, 18 in. to 2 ft.; *Campanula persicifolia*, blue, 2 to 3 ft.; *Campanula persicifolia alba*, white, 2 to 3 ft.; *Campanula persicifolia alba*, fl. pl., white, 2 to 3 ft.; *Campanula carpatica*, blue, 1 ft.; Iris Germanica, various colours, 2 to 3 ft.; *Hemerocallis flava*, yellow, 2 ft.; *Hemerocallis disticha*, fl. pl., bronzy yellow, 3 ft.; Delphiniums, various, 4 to 6 ft.; Single and Double

Comet Aster

Hybrid Pyrethrums, various 2 to 3 ft.; Single and Double Pæonies, various, 2 to 3 ft.; Antirrhinums, various, 1 to 3 ft.

JULY—*Coreopsis lanceolata*, yellow, 3 ft.; *Stenactis speciosa* violet, 3 ft.; *Lathyrus latifolius* pink, 5 to 7 ft.; *Lathyrus latifolius albus*, white, 5 to 7 ft.; *Lupinus polyphyllus*, blue, 3 ft.; *Lupinus polyphyllus albus*, white, 3 ft.; *Campanula grandis alba*, white, 2 ft.; *Campanula Hostii*, blue, 1 ft.; *Lysimachia clethroides*, white, 2 ft.; *Lysimachia vulgaris*, yellow, 2 to 3 ft.; *Lobelia cardinalis*, crimson, 12 to 18 in.; *Helenium pumilum*, yellow, 2 ft.; *Monarda didyma*, scarlet, 3 ft.; *Centranthus ruber*, red and white, 2 ft.; Œnothera taraxacifolia, white, 6 in.; *Funkia japonica aurea folius variegatus*, variegated leaved; *Galega officinalis*, blue, 3 ft.; *Galega officinalis alba*, white, 3 ft.

AUGUST—*Helenium grandicephalum striatum*, yellow and brown, 3 to 4 ft.; *Helianthus multiflorus*, fl. pl., yellow, 4 to 6 ft.; *Helianthus multiflorus major*, yellow, 4 ft.; *Helianthus rigidus* "Miss Mellish," yellow, 6 ft.; *Rudbeckia Newmanii*, orange, 3 ft.; *Eryngium Olivierianum*, blue,

3 ft.; *Echinops ritro*, blue, 3 ft.; *Tradescanthia virginica*, blue and white, 1 ft.; *Galega persica lilacina*, lilac, 3 to 4 ft.; *Polygonum cuspidatum*, white, 4 to 6 ft.; *Polygonum vaccinifolium*, rose, 1 ft.; *Pyrethrum uliginosum*, white, 5 to 6 ft.; *Spiræa aruncus*, white, 3 ft.; *Coreopsis grandiflora*, yellow, 3 ft.

SEPTEMBER—*Aster amellus bessarabicus*, blue, 3 ft.; *Aster Shortii*, blue, 3 ft.; *Aster ericoides*, white, 3 ft.; *Tritoma uvaria*, red, 3 to 4 ft.; *Sedum spectabilis*, pink, 1 ft.; *Anemone japonica*, red, rose, and white, 2 ft.; *Herbaceous Phloxes*, various, 3 ft.; Pampas Grass, white, 4 to 6 ft.; *Helianthus lævis*, yellow, 4 to 6 ft.

OCTOBER—*Schizostylis coccinea*, scarlet, 18 in.; *Aster novæ angliæ*, and *novæ belgiæ*, blue, 3 ft.; *Physalis Alkekengi*, and Franchetti, red fruits, 1 to 2 ft.

NOVEMBER—*Petasites fragrans*, pink, 1 ft.; *Megasea cordifolia*, pink, 1 ft.

DECEMBER—Christmas Roses.

Dianthus

☙ Climbers ❧

For the adornment of dwellings and gardens
By T. W. Sanders, F.L.S., F.R.H.S.

☙ Climbers and Trailers ❧

AN accomplished American gardener, Mr. G. H. Ellwanger says in his charming book, *The Garden's Story*: 'No garden is complete – if a garden can ever be complete – without its flowering climbers; even the kitchen garden should have its scarlet-runner beans, and the front verandah, at least, be festooned with blossoming vines.' We would go farther, and say that no dwelling is complete unless its exterior walls are clothed with the exquisite drapery of the foliage and blossom of the wealth of beautiful climbers that are within the reach of rich and poor in this country. We may, and indeed often do, spend an enormous amount of money and time in fashioning and planting a garden with a beautiful assortment of trees, shrubs, and plants, but if we neglect the all-important point of clothing the walls of our dwellings, or covering those of our gardens with climbers, we make a grievous mistake; in fact, as Mr. Ellwanger in effect says, 'We fail to form a complete garden – a garden beautiful in all its parts, a picture perfect in grace and beauty.' O that men and women who admire and adore all that is beautiful in Nature, would realise the grand importance of this fact, and strive to make not only their garden, but also its immediate surroundings – the exteriors of their dwellings – more ideally beautiful and perfect!

The true art of the gardener is not alone measured by the amount of cultural skill displayed in growing superb examples of vegetables, fruit, or flowers for exhibition, nor by the florid displays of colour in the garden, nor by the intricacy and ingenuity shown in its formation, but by the taste and art displayed in the effective and pleasing adornment of every ugly spot or objectionable feature in the garden and its immediate surroundings.

Creepers and trailers may be roughly divided into several classes. First of all, there are the annual kinds represented by the Canary Creeper, Tall Nasturtium, Tall Convolvulus, Japanese Hop, Morning Glory, *Mina lobata*, and Thunbergias. Then come the herbaceous kinds – White and Pink-flowered. Everlasting Peas, *Calystegia Pubescens flore pleno*, *Convolvulus dahuricus* and *sylvaticus*, *Eccremocarpus scaber*, Common Hop, and *Boussingaultia baselloides*, *Tropæolum speciosum* – so called because their shoots die down to the ground in autumn, new ones appearing in spring. Next we have what are known as evergreen climbers. In this class are included Ivies, Evergreen Firethorn (*Cratægus pyracantha*), *Cotoneaster microphylla*, *Euonymus radicans variegata*, Evergreen Honeysuckle (*Lonicera sempervirens*), *Akebia quinata*, *Berberidopsis corallina*, *Escallonia macrantha floribunda*, and *Smilax aspera*. The fourth and last class contains all those known as deciduous climbers, namely, Clematises in variety, Jasmines, Honeysuckles, Passion Flowers, Virginian Creepers, *Aristolochia sipho* (Dutchman's Pipe), Grape Vines, *Solanum crispum*, Roses,

CONVOLVULUS MINOR.

Tea Tree (*Lycium barbarum*), and Trumpet Flowers (Bignonias).

Some of the kinds in the foregoing list are called twiners because of the natural habit of the shoots to twine or coil themselves round any object near to which they grow. The honeysuckle and hop are examples of twiners. Others, like the ivy, have their branches furnished with tendrils or sucker-like appendages which enable them to cling to walls, &c., for support. These are called creepers. Others again have an upward growth, but yet require artificial support to keep them in position. To this class belong Roses, Clematises, Everlasting Peas, &c. Others possess the property of being easily trained upwards to a wall or fence; or, if allowed to grow naturally, to trail their shoots along the ground, as the Nasturtium, Cotoneaster, &c.

Now, supposing you want to clothe the exterior walls of your dwelling with climbers, the first thing you have to do is to select the kinds suitable for the aspect. Just as all plants will not succeed equally well in sun or in shade in the garden, so will not all creepers thrive satisfactorily in any aspect. Indeed, the great secret of success, in the cultivation of creepers lies in the selection of those kinds that are known to do best in the various aspects. For example, there are few roses that would thrive against an east or a north wall. Variegated ivies, again, never thrive so well against a south as a west wall, and so on. To ensure success, then, you must take special care to select kinds suitable for the various aspects.

For covering a wall facing the south the self-clinging Virginian Creeper (*Ampelopsis Veitchii*) is an excellent plant. This plant requires no training after the first year; it will cling of its own accord to the wall and in a few years cover a large space with deep green foliage in summer, which changes in autumn to the most brilliant of red tints. The Passion Flower (*Passiflora cœrulea*) is another pretty climber. The shoots must, however, be trained as they grow to the wall. Every February shorten the shoots about one-third of their length. There is a white variety of this called Constance Elliott which is equally worthy of being grown. *Wistaria sinensis* is a most beautiful climber for a south wall. It bears large racemes of purplish pea-shaped flowers and has very prettily divided pale green leaves. The shoots require to be trained as they grow to the wall. Each year, in February, prune the previous year's shoots back to within an inch of their base. Then there are numerous kinds of Clematis which are adapted for a south wall. The best of these are Beauty of Worcester, Lady Caroline Nevill, Mrs. James Bateman, Princess of Wales, Duchess of

A lady in her conservatory, c. 1890

Edinburgh, and Henryi. All these require to be trained to the wall and to have their previous year's shoots shortened one-third in February. The Yellow Jasmine (*Jasminum nudiflorum*), which flowers during the winter, is also a good plant for a south wall. In warm and sheltered districts *Bignonia radicans*, bearing reddish orange flowers; *Escallonia macrantha floribunda*, a plant with dark green foliage and small red flowers, to be seen growing against almost every cottage in the Isle of Wight; *Berberidopsis corallina*, evergreen, with pretty drooping crimson flowers; *Solanum crispum*, bearing bunches of pale lavender potato-like flowers; *Magnolia grandiflora*, another evergreen with handsome white flowers; and Ceanothus azureus, bearing spikes of pale blue blossoms, are all worthy of cultivation. If you have a fancy for roses, grow Madame Berard, fleshy pink; Gloire de Dijon, buff; W. A. Richardson, orange; Reine Marie Henriette, crimson; and Maréchal Niel, yellow – all deliciously fragrant tea scented roses.

Nor is our list of plants for a south wall yet exhausted. Those who have a greenhouse and can raise plants easily from seed are advised to grow *Eccremocarpus scaber* (Chilian Glory Flower), *Cobæa scandens* (Cup and Saucer Flower), *Tropæolum Lobbianum* (Lobb's Nasturtium), *Mina lobata* and *Thunbergia alata*. The *Eccremocarpus* will, in dry soils, survive the winter and put forth vigorous shoots in spring. All the others, however, must be treated as annuals and raised from seed each year. Those who cannot raise the latter plants from seed, nor purchase those previously referred to, may get a good display by sowing seeds of the many kinds of Tall Nasturtiums, Convolvulus, and Canary Creeper in the soil at the base of the wall in April.

As to walls facing west, variegated ivies will do well here, and so will *Clematis Jackmanii*, purple, flowering in August; *Clematis montana*, white, blooming in spring; *Jasminum officinale*, white; *Cydonia Mauleii*, bearing crimson apple-like blossoms in spring; *Chimonanthus fragrans*, yielding deliciously fragrant flowers in winter; Dutch Honeysuckle; Claret-leaved Grape Vine (*Vitis vinifera purpurea*), having leaves of a rich claret shade of colour; *Fuchsia Ricartonii*, *gracilis* and *macrostema globosa*; *Garrya elliptica*, an evergreen plant bearing greyish catkins, and very pretty; *Berberis stenophylla*, orange flowered and evergreen; *Ampelopsis*

Veitchii, already referred to in connection with creepers for a south wall; *Euonymus radicans variegata*, silvery-leaved; and any of the roses mentioned for the south aspect form a selection of really pretty climbers for a west aspect. If cheaper plants are required, the Canary Creeper, Nasturtium, Scarlet Runner Bean, and the Variegated Japanese Hop, or the Pink or White flowered Everlasting Peas may be substituted for the foregoing permanent climbers.

For east walls there is not such a variety of plants to choose from. Here the Evergreen and the Ayrshire Roses (*Félicité perpétué*, Longworth Rambler, and the Dundee Rambler); the common Virginian Creeper (*Ampelopsis hederacea*); *Cydonia japonica*, crimson flowering in spring; green ivies; *Cratægus Lelandii*, evergreen, bearing orange-red berries in winter; *Cotoneaster microphylla*, also evergreen and orange berried in winter; and

Forsythia suspensa, yellow flowered and spring flowering, are th
best kinds for this aspect. To this list the Canary Creeper, Tal
Nasturtium, and Japanese Hop may be added as cheap and easil
grown kinds.

Against a wall facing north, green ivies – especially Rœgner'
Ivy – Virginian Creeper, Boursalt Rose (*Amadis*); America
Allspice (*Calycanthus macrophyllum*); *Cratægus pyracantha*; Te
Tree (*Lycium barbarum*); and *Clematis flammula*, white, bloomin
in autumn, are the only kinds we can recommend. The Tal
Nasturtium and the Japanese Hop frequently do well in such
position. In the northern, cooler and moister parts of the kingdon
the beautiful Flame Flower (*Tropæolum speciosum*) succeed
admirably against a north wall. In Scotland it may often be me
with thriving luxuriantly and flowering profusely against cottag
walls. In the south it rarely succeeds unless grown in a deep mois
bed of peat, leaf mould, and sand, against a cool north wall. It wil
not succeed in hot positions, nor in dry soils. The roots should b
planted in October.

So much for the house walls. Now we will turn our attentio
more particularly to the garden, and say something about climber
for arches, &c. Supposing the reader wishes to cover a wire arc
with some climber, he cannot do better than plant a *Clemati
Jackmanii*; an Evergreen, Gloire de Dijon, or a Madame Berard te
rose; a *Convolvulus sylvatica*, white and pink flowered; *Calystegi
pubescens flore-pleno* (Double Convolvulus); *Lonicera caprifoliun*
(Honeysuckle); *Jasminum nudiflorum* (Winter flowering Jasmine)
or the Evergreen Firethorn (*Cratægus pyracantha*). Either o
these will form excellent permanent climbers. The Commor
Hop (*Humulus lupulus*) and the Pink Everlasting Pea (*Lathyru
latifolius*) are often used with great success for the same purpose

All these are permanent plants. For temporary effect in summer, *Tropæolum Lobbianum* and any of the excellent varieties of Tall Nasturtiums offered for sale in the 'One & All' Seed Catalogue issued by the Agricultural and Horticultural Association; the Canary Creeper, the green and variegated sorts of the Japanese Hop (*Humulus Japonicus*); Tall Convolvulus (*Convolvulus major*); also *Cobæa scandens*, a greenhouse plant, which may be grown outdoors in summer, and *Clianthus Dampieri* may be employed with success for decorating arches in summer.

In small gardens there are often ugly objects which it is desirable to hide from view during the summer. Among such objects the dust bin, water butt, dog kennel, rubbish corner, or entrance to an outdoor w.c. are familiar examples. A temporary framework of pea sticks, bean stakes, or timber may be erected; or, better still,

Ladies in the garden, c. 1900

a lattice-work trellis may be fixed up and painted green. If th
position does not get much sun the green or Japanese Hop or th
Tall Nasturtium may be used for covering the trellis or framework
If sunny, use the Canary Creeper, Tall Convolvulus, Scarlet Runne
Bean, *Tropæolum Lobbianum* or the Tall Nasturtium. Wher
permanent climbers are preferred the Virginian Creeper is th
best plant for a shady spot, and the Common Hop, Everlasting Pea
Clematis Jackmanii, *Clematis montana*, *Jasminum nudiflorum*, an
the following roses: Crimson Rambler, Flora, Dundee Ramble
and The Garland.

For a sunny arbour there is nothing to equal a combinatio
of *Clematis montana*, *Clematis Jackmanii*, *Jasminum nudiflorum*
Honeysuckle; Gloire de Dijon, Madame Berard, and Flora rose

Forsythia suspensa, *Berberis stenophylla*, Claret-leaved Vine and *Aristolochia sipho*. Any or all of these will make splendid permanent climbers. To the list may be added the Common Hop and the Everlasting Pea. Of temporary climbers, the Tall Nasturtium, *Tropæolum Lobbianum*, Canary Creeper, *Cobæa scandens*, *Eccremocarpus scaber*, and the green and variegated Japanese Hop may be used with good effect.

Then for covering garden fences, what can be more beautiful than many of the free-growing and free-flowering roses? Such sorts as Dundee Rambler, *Félicité perpétué*, Rampant, Queen of the Belgians, and The Garland, are absolutely unsurpassable for the purpose. If to these we add the Everlasting Peas, Double Convolvulus, Japanese Quince (*Cydonia japonica*), *Jasminum nudiflorum*, and many of those advised for walls, we shall have a good selection of beautiful plants that will greatly improve the appearance of any fence they are grown against. The cottager or artisan whose means will not allow him to purchase roses or permanent climbers may get a great deal of pleasure and add greatly to the attractiveness of his garden by cultivating Runner Beans, Nasturtiums, and Canary Creepers against his fences.

Pansies

by James B. Riding, F.R.H.S

THIS beautiful flower has developed remarkably during the past forty years; so much so, indeed, that it bears little resemblance to the original species, Viola tricolor, which is so common in many British cornfields. The modern race is an abiding monument to those florists who, by years of selection and intercrossing, presented us with the Show and Fancy sections so much esteemed twenty or thirty years ago. Now, however, our tastes and fashions are broader than they were a generation ago, and we see the rigid formality in the old flowers giving place to greater freedom.

The pansy lover of to-day does not concern himself very much as to whether the flowers are circular, smooth, and flat, and strictly in accord with the rules of the old florists, but demands varieties which will make beautiful displays in the beds and borders of the garden. Still, we respect the splendid work of the florists, for had they not raised the flower to its wonderful standard by years of unremitting and strenuous work, we should not have been able to produce the type so popular at the present time. There can be little doubt that the persistent intercrossing is responsible for the weakly habit of the show pansy today. So much has this brought the plants into disrepute that their culture is practically confined to a few growers in the Midlands, Northern Counties, and Scotland, while in the South, where they were for many years of last century largely and successfully grown, they are comparatively seldom seen.

☙ The Fancy Pansy ☙

This was evolved from the show type at a later date by the Continental florists, who introduced the bright colours and larger size in the blooms, at the same time producing plants of much stronger habit and with far hardier constitutions. The Continental varieties introduced were at once taken in hand by our own growers, who quickly added the essentials to raise it to the florists' standard. The result is that today the fancy pansy is as perfect in form as the older type, and is judged on precisely the same lines. Although extremely popular in the Midlands and the North, the florists' forms of fancy pansies cannot claim the esteem in which those raised from seed are held throughout the country. These are raised in millions each year, and prove a source of enjoyment to as many people. For what is more fascinating than watching the unfolding petals of a bed of good seedling pansies?

☙ Violas or Tufted Pansies ☙

This popular section is said to have been the result of a cross between the show pansy and *Viola cornuta*, and it is the most esteemed for bedding or massing purposes. Formerly the flowers were all self colours, but now they have been crossed to secure larger flowers and a greater range of coloration, with the result that to-day we have scores of varieties, most of them useful for decorative effect, while a small minority only are suitable for the show board or exhibition table. The earlier forms were of dwarf, bushy habit, but many of the modern sorts have the growth of the fancy pansy, which does not add to their usefulness or charm as garden flowers. Their long season of flowering makes them general favourites and accounts for the position they now hold in our gardens. The rayless varieties are particularly attractive, and the majority possess a fine tufted habit.

❧ Miniature Violas ❧

These are commonly known as the Violetta type, and are the result of a cross between a bedding pansy and *Viola cornuta*. The plants are very dwarf and tufted in growth, and the flowers small and dainty. The plants are remarkably free flowering, though rather late in starting; they are especially charming for edgings and are equally suitable for rockeries. It is, perhaps, superfluous to add that they are being improved in all respects.

❧ The Planting Period ❧

This may extend over a long period according to the nature of the soil, the situation of the garden, or other local circumstance, and each grower must make his own final decision. I prefer planting the seedlings in October or November, so that they may obtain a thorough grip of the soil before the very severe weather starts. As a general rule they will pass through a hard winter without any protection whatever, and make splendid plants for early flowering in the following year. I am now alluding to gardens which enjoy the pure country air and not to those less fortunately situated near large towns or cities, or even where fogs are very prevalent. I would advise all growers who labour under these conditions to winter the seedlings in cold-frames. The pansy is perfectly hardy, but it will not stand the sooty deposit so prevalent in such districts during the winter months. Provided that they are protected from this, and also from excessive moisture, they will pass through the winter quite safely.

I might mention, in passing, that the majority of amateur gardeners procure their plants from the florists' shops or costers' barrows in the spring when they have just produced their first flowers, and attracted by their enormous size and brilliant colours they purchase them and plant them out without delay. What is the result? Simply that each succeeding flower is smaller than its predecessor, and the buyer soon becomes disgusted with his purchase. This deterioration in the flowers is due primarily to the check the plant receives in lifting and 'balling up'; an operation that means squeezing the soil in a ball with the hand until it is quite firm (in some instances they are balled in clay with a view to keeping them fresh until they are disposed of by the vendor). This treatment is most prejudicial to the well-being of the plant, since in many cases the roots are locked in a prison from which they never escape, with the natural result the plants drag on a miserable existence for a month or two and then collapse through sheer exhaustion. Far better is it when such stuff has to be handled to partially release the roots so that they can work out into the soil without let or hindrance. If this simple detail were only carried out, we should not see half the poor, miserable plants we meet with daily in the early summer months. Planting should be done when the soil is neither too wet nor too dry, but in such a condition that the cultivator can plant firmly without squeezing out the air.

A houseowner and his gardener, c. 1910

➷ Propagation ❧

Pansies are readily increased by division, cuttings, or seeds. The vast majority are raised from seeds, except in the case of named varieties, which must necessarily be increased by division or cuttings, since the seedlings cannot be relied upon to come true. The same remarks apply equally to the "tufted" pansy or viola. We have, then, three methods to consider.

1. Division – The division of the plants is more readily carried out in the case of the viola than the pansy, for the habit of the former lends itself peculiarly to the method. No doubt the division of the plants during October and November is the most simple form of propagation, since it merely consists of lifting the plant, pulling it asunder in a number of small pieces with the roots attached, and replanting at once in the stations or beds prepared for them. Could anything be easier? These plants,

Pansy cuttings in box

too, will flower earlier in the spring than those produced from cuttings, though perhaps they do not produce the fine flowers which we get from stock raised from cuttings.

2. Cuttings – All named varieties of both pansies and violas are generally increased by this method. The young shoots or growths from the base of the plants will root readily at almost any period, but the rule is to take them during the months of July and August for October and November planting, while those required for spring planting can be taken during September and October; further propagation can be carried out early in the spring months with success should the occasion for doing so arise.

With cuttings in frames, in most districts it is best to root the cuttings in cold-frames, as they are then more under the control of the grower. For example, the cuttings which are taken in the months of July and August will require a slight shade during the day, and this is most readily applied by using shaded lights which can be put on at will, always tilting them to allow plenty of air. In the evening they should be removed to allow the cuttings to become saturated with dew. This will keep them erect and check the red spider, which is always a troublesome pest at this season of the year. As soon as the cuttings are rooted they should be

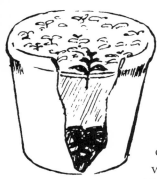

Pansy cuttings in pot

fully exposed, and will give the grower no further trouble.

With Cuttings in the open air, in propagation may be readily carried out in the open air provided that we can give them a shady position, such as under a north wall or hedge – in fact, any situation where they will escape the direct influence of the sun. The cuttings root just as readily out of doors as they do in frames. Naturally the soil must be kept moist, and the cuttings sprinkled over each evening if they droop. Under these conditions the amateur can raise or increase his stock to any desired extent.

3. Seed – There are pansies and pansies, just in the same way as there are horses and horses, and the more highly bred they become the more difficult they are to reproduce. The common Pansies readily produce seed, but not so the highest results of the florist's art; the gorgeous colours and immense size of flowers which have been evolved by crossing and selection during the past twenty years have given us a race of flowers that produce very little seed. The energies of the plant have been so developed to produce size and colour that the plant becomes more or less exhausted before

the essential organs are developed, with the natural result that they fail to reproduce themselves in any quantity. From a commercial point of view, therefore, the choicest strains of Pansies will always be somewhat expensive.

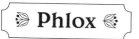

Phlox

By Charles H. Curtis, F.R.H.S.

THESE handsome, bold, and bright flowers occupy such a high position in Flora's realm that a garden without Herbaceous Phloxes is unthinkable. The sturdy stems rise from eighteen inches to rather more than four feet high, according to the variety, though one or two varieties of comparatively recent introduction are lowly enough to form a carpeting or edging to the others. The leafage forms a fine setting for the large branching panicles of flowers that are carried erect at the summit of each growth, but the size and greenness of the foliage, as well as the size of the head of bloom, and the size and brilliance or purity of the individual flowers, are all determined by the degree of cultivation afforded. Even the old-fashioned varieties, with small flowers and lax flower-heads, may become plants of great beauty if thoroughly well grown, while the very finest example of the florist's skill – the last word in Phloxes – may be spoiled and made useless and unbeautiful by poor soil and inattention to a few simple cultural details. The person who always complains and asserts that his or her non-success is due to the old varieties grown is like the unskilful

workman who endeavours to hide his ignorance and inability by constantly grumbling at and blaming his tools.

Even a casual observer will notice that Herbaceous Phloxes do not all flower at the same period, and it is this difference of the flowering time that naturally separates the varieties into two sections. These are the Early-flowering or *Suffruticosa* section and the Late-flowering or *Decussata* section. But the line of demarcation between the two sections grows fainter year by year. The later members of the early section mingle their blooms with those of the early members of the late section, and our gardens are the gainers, because now it is possible to have Phloxes blooming in succession from early summer until autumn is well advanced.

❧ A Selection of Early-flowering Phlox ❧

Attraction, 2½ ft., white, crimson centre.

Burns, 1½ ft., rosy-violet.

Charles J. Moir, 2 ft., white, pale pink centre.

Harry Veitch, 2 ft., creamy white, crimson centre.

Herbert Cutbush, 2 ft., white, pink centre.

Isaac House, 2½ ft., silvery pink.

James Hunter, 2 ft., deep rose, darker centre.

Ladysmith, 1½ ft., cream white, crimson centre.

Maggie Forbes, 1½ ft., white, crimson centre.

Magnificence, 1½ ft., rose pink, crimson centre.

Miss Lingard, 3 ft., white, lilac centre, very fine.

Mrs. Cobham, 1½ ft., white and pink.

Mrs. Forbes, 2 ft., pure white.

Mrs. Jas. Robertson, 2 ft., rosy-lilac, deeper eye.

Perfection, 2 ft., white, deep pink centre.

Prince, 2½ ft., white, rose pink centre.

Snowflake, 1½ ft., pure white.

The Queen, 3 ft., soft delicate pink, deeper centre.

❧ A Selection of Late-flowering Phlox ❧

Amazone, 3½ ft., pure white.

Archibald Forbes, 2 ft., rosy salmon, crimson centre.

Armand Dayot, 2 ft., salmon, lilac centre.

Belle Alliance, 3 ft., white, rosy centre.

Boule de Feu, 2½ ft., scarlet.

Brilliant, 2 ft., salmon, rosy centre.

Camille Desmoulins, 2 ft., rosy violet, white centre.

Charles Pfitzer, 2 ft., rosy pink, paler centre.

Coccinea, 4 ft., vermilion.

Cœur de Lion, 4 ft., rose purple, carmine centre.

Coquelicot, 3 ft., orange scarlet.

Crépuscule, 3 ft., pale lilac, mauve centre.

Duhamel, 3 ft., bright red.

Eclaireur, 3 ft., carmine, buff centre.

Edward Bour, 2 ft., red-purple.

Espérance, 3 ft., deep rose pink, white centre.

Etienne Lamy, 2½ ft., salmon, crimson centre.

Etna, 3½ ft., bright orange scarlet.

Eugene Danzanvilliers, 3 ft., bright lilac, white centre.

Fedora, 2½ ft., rose and white.

Flocon de Neige, 2½ ft., white.

FreifrÄulein G. von Lassberg, 2½ ft., white.

Flambeau, 2½ ft., bright scarlet.

Henry Fouquier, 3 ft., rose, crimson centre.

Henri Marcel, 3 ft., carmine, rosy centre.

Iris, 3 ft., bright violet, blue-purple centre.

John Forbes, 4 ft., pink, crimson centre.

John Fraser, 3 ft., rich salmon, paler centre.

La Neige, 2 ft., pure white.

Le Mahdi, 3 ft., deep violet purple.

Le Prophete, 3 ft., dark mauve, red centre.

Liberté, 3½ ft., light orange, carmine centre.

Lord Kelvin, 3½ ft., bright red, crimson centre.

Lord Rayleigh, 3 ft., violet, purple centre.

Louis Blanc, 3 ft., violet, dark centre.

Maximilian, 3½ ft., orange scarlet, crimson centre.

Mrs. Burn, 3 ft., orange scarlet, crimson centre.

Mrs. Oliver, 2½ ft., rose pink, white centre.

Obélisque, 3 ft., deep rose, crimson centre.

Panthéon, 3 ft., salmon.

Papillon, 2½ ft., bluish lilac.

Paul Bert, 4 ft., lilac, violet centre.

Paul Fliche, 2½ ft., soft rose.

Rossignol, 2½ ft., mauve, white centre.

Sarabande, 3 ft., rosy carmine, white centre.

Sheriff Ivory, 4 ft., rose, crimson centre.

Siebold, 3 ft., rich red, rose centre.

Tapis Blanc, 1 ft., white.

Tom Welsh, 4 ft., rich carmine.

Tunisie, 2½ ft., violet and purple.

Wm. Robinson, 4 ft., salmon, violet centre.

Zouave, 3 ft., dark magenta.

✑ Antirrhinums ✑

✑ The Plants in Beds ✑

AS a bedding plant to provide a display of flowers during late summer and early autumn the Phlox is surpassed by few. Before we proceed, further attention must be drawn to the three distinct types of the plant, *viz.*, tall, medium, and dwarf. The first-named grows from 2 feet 6 inches to 3 feet high in well-cultivated soil, the dwarf 1 foot, and the medium about half way between the two, a varied assortment of colours being found in each type, and to which attention will be drawn later. The tall varieties will need staking and tying.

Generally speaking, the medium and dwarf types are best for beds, although where very large, isolated beds are to be filled, and a bold display is desired, the tall, medium, and dwarf varieties may all be employed. It is preferable to fill a bed with Antirrhinums alone; combined with other plants, half their beauty is lost. Naturally the colours employed will depend upon individual taste, but I would warn anyone against employing an indiscriminate mixture of colours in one bed. Where a bold display is to be made, I am in favour of using one colour, or shades of a colour, only in a bed, and in such a case, of course, any of the colours available may be chosen. A good and striking mixture is deep rich crimson and white. Thus the centre of the bed might be filled with a crimson variety belonging to the medium type, and this surrounded with a broad band of a dwarf white sort. The beautiful terracotta and delicate pink shades go well together, but other colours ought not to be mixed with them. Yellow is a difficult colour to use in beds, and should either be kept by itself or used in conjunction with white.

Antirrhinums as Border Plants

For filling up blank spaces in the mixed or herbaceous border, the various types of the Antirrhinum are of considerable value. Generally speaking the medium and tall forms are best for this purpose, but where gaps occur near the front of the border, the dwarf varieties may sometimes be used to advantage. Where groups of such bulbs as Daffodils and Tulips are grown in the border, the Antirrhinums may be planted between them, so that by the time the foliage of the bulbs is dead, the

Antirrhinum triste, Melancholy or Black-Flowered Toad-flax

Snapdragons will have formed sturdy plants, and have filled what would otherwise have been a blank space.

When planting in borders it is advisable to allow a little more space, say 3 inches for each type, between the plants than advised for beds, as it is not so essential or desirable that the plants shall form a close mass of foliage and flowers. The same attention to the arrangement of the various colours must be given, and it will also be necessary to bear in mind the colours of the flowers of other plants close by that are likely to be open at the same time.

Antirrhinums in Window-boxes and Tubs

Even those who do not possess beds and borders in which to grow the Snapdragons need not despair, as they can be successfully grown in window-boxes and tubs, even in large towns, and possess the advantage of thriving in soil that would be too poor for the welfare of many other plants. The boxes or tubs should be well drained by placing some pieces of broken pots, bricks, or, failing these, rough stones or even cinders over the holes in the bottom, then put some rough soil over these, and subsequently fill up with the best soil obtainable. For preference it should consist of good loam two parts and coarse sand and old mortar half a part each. Whatever soil is used the incorporation of some old mortar will benefit the plants. Usually the dwarf or medium varieties are best for the purposes named, and it is advisable to keep one colour, or shades of a colour, together.

Antirrhinums in Walls

Where an old stone or brick wall is available this will form an ideal situation for growing the Snapdragon in a natural and semi-wild manner, and once the plants are established, they may usually be relied upon to reproduce themselves year after year. The medium and dwarf varieties are best for the purpose, and a good mixture will generally give the most pleasure, although, of course, individual taste must be considered. In any case do not choose named varieties, as these are generally highly bred, and do not possess the same vigour as ordinary seedlings.

The best means of establishing these plants on old walls is undoubtedly by seeds, and these should be sown in August or September. The joints between the stones or bricks may have a little of the mortar dug out with a cold chisel or an old knife, and, although the plants can be made to grow in the side of the wall near the top, they usually do better on the top itself. Holes two inches deep will suffice, and into these some good ordinary potting soil should be rammed rather firmly. After this is done a few seeds may be sown in each hole, pressed well into the soil, and then left to take their chance. The colours of the flowers of plants growing in walls always appear to me to be richer than those of similar varieties growing in cultivated soil.

❧ The Rose ❦

By Hon. H. A. Stanhope

WILLS'S CIGARETTES.

Hugh Dickson.

THE lavish use of roses by the luxurious Romans in their feasts led the early Christians to discourage at first what had been so closely associated with effeminate voluptuousness. Yet the rose soon became once more surrounded by sacred legends and traditions. In the old Scandinavian mythology the rose had been held sacred to Hulda, as in Rome to Venus and Hymen. But Christianity, as happened in other cases, adopted and gave a new meaning to old-world customs. Thus the rose came to be regarded as the special flower of the Virgin Mary. Roses were said to have sprung beneath her feet. Tradition reported that roses and lilies were found in her tomb after her assumption into heaven. The month of May, which, in the old mythology, had been Maia's month, became the month of the Madonna, and pious Roman Catholic folk keep roses in the oratory all that month. Both white and red roses were assigned to the festival of the Visitation of our Lady (July 2nd), whilst on St. Mary Magdalen's day (July 22nd) roses were said to fade. The Virgin Mary was called the Rose of Roses, the Rose of Grace and Sweetness; and the Italian poet Dante speaks of "The Rose in which the Divine word was made flesh."

With some truth it might be said that:

Roses, then,
First seen on earth since Paradise was lost,
Profusely bloom around her white and red,
In all their rich variety of hues.

At St. Peter's, in Rome, there was formerly, on mid-Lent Sunday, the ceremony of blessing the golden rose, which was afterwards sent by the Pope, as a sign of special favour, to some distinguished prince. Thus one was given to Louis VII. of France, afterwards to a Doge of Venice, to the Emperor Sigismund, to our Henry VI., and, curiously enough, on two occasions to Henry VIII.

There was also a quaint custom in France; lasting until the sixteenth century, called the *Baillée des Roses* – a tribute of roses from the peers of France to the Parliament, when sitting in April, May and June.

Then we find that in London, Ely House, Holborn, was let on lease for 21 years to Sir Christopher Hatton, for a rent of red roses, the right being given to the lessor of gathering 20

WILLS'S CIGARETTES.

Lady Hillingdon.

bushels of roses every year. To this day the Warden of St. Olave's School in London receives a bouquet of roses as rent of a piece of land, which was leased in 1656 for 'a term of 500 years', at the yearly rent of a red rose payable at midsummer if lawfully demanded.

In ancient times the rose was valued for the wonderful effects which were attributed to its use in medicine. Preparations of roses were supposed to be useful in hydrophobia, in toothache, earache, in internal troubles, in faintness, and for external wounds, as well as for many other human ills. Homer, even in his day, speaks of 'applying sovereign force of rosy balms.' The great Arabic philosopher Avicenna (AD 980–1037), styled the 'Prince of Physicians', also advocates their use. What further magical effects were sometimes expected may be gathered from the following old recipe:– 'Mix oil of roses with a grain of mustard, a weasel's foot, olive oil and sulphur anoint your house with this during sunshine, and the whole house will appear on fire.' More wonderful still, Apuleius, in his novel makes a donkey become a man on eating roses!

It is curious to note the various ancient legendary accounts given of the origin of red roses. It used to be said that white roses became red from the blood of Adonis, slain by a wild boar; but the Latin poet Catullus says they became red from having pricked the foot of Venus hastening to her loved one. Then there is the tale that Cupid, in dancing, upset a bowl of heavenly nectar, and thus first dyed roses.

Very numerous are the legends connected with the rose, some of them pure fairy tales, such as the Italian story of the *Rosa Fatata* (enchanted), when a merchant, being asked by his daughter to bring her a rose tree as a present, goes one day to a garden and selects one, when a monster appears, obliges him to return with his daughter, with whom the monster then falls in love; on her promising to marry him he becomes a handsome prince, each rose tree a city, and so on; for he had been enchanted, and the spell could only be broken when he should be redeemed by the love of a maiden.

Dreams of roses were said to foretell long life and happiness; of withered roses unhappiness and death. If on earth Venus herself finds a rival in the rose, the eternal heaven in which she was supposed to dwell has been called 'the garden of roses.' It is surely not the fear of withering blooms or of fleeting beauty which inspired that last thought, but rather Shakespeare's happy reminder of lovely roses that 'Of their sweet deaths are sweetest odours made.'

PART III

The Allotment
and Vegetable Plot

The Allotment
and Vegetable Plot

Encouragement of productive vegetable and fruit growing for the suppor
of working-class families was one of the main thrusts of the cooperative
movements overseen by Edward Owen Greening, and this interest is
strongly reflected in the 'One & All' garden books. Having lured in hi
readers with promises of Sweet Peas and Annuals flowers, Greening
produced a booklet on simple salad vegetables before moving swiftly
on to the more serious side of vegetable production, with 'Vegetables'
(Booklet No. 4), 'Manuring' (No. 6), 'Potatoes' (No. 7) and 'Allotments'
(No. 8). Pausing for light relief with 'Rose's and 'Weather' (No. 9 and No
12), books 13, 15, 16 and 17 again returned to the productive side of
gardening, covering onions, peas, tomatoes and beans. Pausing to cover
in more detail the 'Roots' and 'Cabbages' first seen in the more general
work on vegetables, Greening then returned to allotments (and the
allotment 'movement' more generally), in Nos. 27 and 28 (the latter a
double edition). This concern, predating the productivity campaigns of
the First World War, reflected nineteenth-century changes both in the
countryside (where enclosures had resulted in loss of land available to
the rural labourer), and in the towns (where a vastly increased working
and middle-class population had been left with no means of producing
their own food). Greening (through his chosen writer T. W. Sanders) had
covered the more recent history of the allotment movement in the firs
of his booklets on the subject – but his campaigning zeal for the provision

and efficient use of allotments and vegetable plots for all shines through each of the 'allotment' booklets. His suggestion of allotment gardens for soldiers in barracks pre-dates by decades a similar scheme put in place by the government in the Second World War. Booklet 28 on cropping allotments, dealing with the layout of the plot and the use of techniques such as inter-cropping and crop rotation, can be used as an exact model by present-day allotment holders, although the outline of suitable rules and regulations for allotments, including the exhortation that 'No work shall be done on Sundays after 10 am' is perhaps less likely to meet with enthusiasm, as religious observance has fallen dramatically. It is however satisfying to find that the basics of sowing, tending and cropping were much the same then as they are now; and if Salsify, Scorzonera and Seakale (No. 4) play a less prominent role in our vegetable diet than was the case for the Edwardians perhaps it is time for their revival!

Twigs Way

Allotments

By T. W. Sanders, F.L.S., F.R.H.S.

THE "three acres and a cow" problem that startled rural England some years ago, and became the precursor of the Allotment Act of 1887, is now a matter of ancient history. No question was probably held up to more ridicule than this. The idea of providing every rustic with three acres and a cow unfortunately for its author, fell to the ground, but it produced one good result, the passing of the Allotment Act, by means of which country dwellers are enabled, through the medium of the Sanitary, District, or Parish Councils, to obtain plots of land for gardening purposes. But it is not an easy matter to put the Act in force; and hence many, while anxious to avail themselves of the benefit of the Act, hesitate to put its cumbrous and costly machinery into motion.

Fortunately it is not a *sine qua non* in all cases where land is desired for allotments that applicants should avail themselves of the provisions of the Allotment Acts to obtain it. If it were so, then we fear allotments in the neighbourhood of towns would not be so numerous as they are at the present time. In saying this, we must not be understood as depreciating the value of the Acts. They are no doubt of considerable service where land cannot be obtained by a friendly arrangement between owners and applicants; but we say most emphatically that their provisions should only be resorted to as a last resource.

In the neighbourhood of the Metropolis there are numerous allotment gardens that have been obtained in a friendly way

Chippenham allotments, c. 1910

and which are carried on most successfully. Some of these are laid out in twenty-five rod plots, and let by the owner direct to each occupier on a yearly tenancy at one shilling per statute rod per annum. These occur on Lord Northbrook's estate at Lee, Kent In another case, land is hired by a responsible and philanthropic gentleman from one of the City companies in the neighbourhood of Catford, Kent, and by him sublet in small plots to worthy applicants on the same terms as the preceding case. The gentleman in question makes only an infinitesimal profit out of the sublet plots, and this is placed to a general fund for repairs, making roads, keeping fences in order, and providing prizes for encouraging the occupiers to keep their plots well cropped and in good order.

Allotment Rules

1. Every person before becoming a tenant must be duly elected a member of the Society, and have paid his subscription. He will not be eligible to participate in the ballot for ground, until one clear month from the date of payment of subscription to the Society.

2. Rent shall be at the maximum charge or sixpence per rod per annum, payable in advance at Midsummer. Each tenant shall be provided with a rent-book free. Any tenant losing the same shall be charged threepence: for a new one, which he must provide himself with forthwith.

3. No plot shall be sublet.

4. No work shall be done on Sundays after 10 a.m.

5. No building of any kind shall be erected on the ground, and no bush fruit or rose trees be planted less than three feet from the paths.

6. No fencing shall be removed without the consent of the Allotment Committee.

7. No dogs, perambulators, or children of tender ages shall be admitted, unless under proper control.

8. No rubbish of any kind shall be deposited in the public road or footpath.

9. Each tenant shall give twelve inches around his allotment to form a path, which must be twenty-four inches wide.

10. Each tenant must keep his ground in proper cultivation, also use his best endeavours to protect the fences and his neighbour's produce, and keep in repair the paths adjoining his plot.

11. Each tenant shall not cause, but endeavour to prevent, any nuisance which may arise from burning rubbish, or manuring his ground, &c.

12. Each tenant shall be provided with a key, and shall not enter the ground except by the gates provided, and on entering or leaving it must leave the gate securely locked. Any tenant having in his possession the padlock of any gate shall be fined 2s. 6d.

13. Any tenant wishing to give up possession of his ground shall give three months' notice, in writing, to the Secretary, such notice to expire at Lady Day, and at the expiration of the tenancy the key shall be delivered up to the Secretary. Any tenant losing his key must provide himself with another forthwith, for which he will be charged sixpence.

14. Should any plot or plots be required for any purposes compensation shall be settled by arbitration, according to the terms of agreement held by the Society from the Lessors.

15. All the above rules shall be strictly enforced and be binding on the tenants, and the Society shall have the right of re-entry and possession of the ground, without any notice or compensation, either for non-payment of rent, or for breach or non-performance of any of them.

16. Any question not provided for by these rules shall be decided by the Allotment Committee (elected from the General Committee), who shall report the same to the General Committee for final decision.

OUR ALLOTMENT OUTFIT.

Another instance of voluntary allotments is to be seen in that erstwhile swamp, the Isle of Dogs. Here was formerly a large tract of waste ground, at one time used as a deposit for sanitary refuse, and now, through the influence of Mr. John MacDougall, L.C.C., and a band of willing and enthusiastic workers, converted into a huge garden, laid out in small plots, and cultivated by residents - working-men – in the neighbourhood. When first started, and, for aught we know to the contrary is the case now, stable-keepers in the district used to pay the allotment committee sixpence per oad for the privilege of depositing the manure from their stables on the ground.

And then, to take another case with which we are very familiar, the allotments held under the auspices of the Ladywell and District Horticultural Society, a society composed mainly of working-men. Some of the members were able to obtain small plots of ground in the neighbourhood, and to grow excellent produce, which invariably gained leading prizes at the Society's exhibitions. Their success and opportunities made other less fortunate members yearn for similar plots, and stimulated the executive to

THE ALLOTMENT
· HOLDERS · DREAM ·

MARROWS CABBAGE PEAS CARROTS PARSNIPS
POTATOES   ONIONS TURNIPS
                                BEANS

If only this sweet dream of mine
Will one day turn out true,
I'll gather all the best I can
And send along to you.

take steps to see if it were possible to obtain land under the auspices of the Society. An opportunity at length arose, in the shape of some four acres of land awaiting building operations in Lewisham Park, the property of the Right Hon. the Earl of Dartmouth, the Lord of the Manor of Lewisham. His lordship was approached on the subject of acquiring this land, if only on short tenure, for allotments, and he readily assented to its being leased to the Society at the nominal rental of threepence per rod per annum.

There are numbers of other societies in and about London and other towns who might imitate this good example with benefit to themselves and hundreds of working-men, who would only be too glad to have a plot of ground in, which to grow a few vegetables for themselves and families. Waste land, lying idle and unprofitable, and awaiting building operations, might, with a little tact and diplomacy, be secured on short tenure from landowners in the district. Such land would lose nothing by being cultivated, in fact would be greatly improved, and at the same time be conferring a great benefit on artisans and working-men generally. It is of little use, however, applying to landowners for individual plots; they do not care to be bothered with a number of small tenants. It is far better for a number to co-operate together, form a small society, and in this collective or corporate capacity apply for the land, agree to pay the rent in one sum, and sublet and collect the rents from the holders of the plots. Such a society, formed and worked on co-operative lines, could do more; it could undertake to purchase its manures, seeds, and tools, and if necessary lay on water, at a considerable saving in outlay.

Approach the local clergy and leading residents in a diplomatic manner, tell them your wants, and if there is land to be had, and you go the right way to work, you will get it. Never mind about insecurity of tenure. If you are only able to secure a plot for one year, another will turn up somewhere else. The pleasure of growing your own vegetables for the pot, and maybe a few flowers for the wife to deck her home with, coupled with the beneficial exercise and the healthy occupation of turning over the soil, will more than repay for your trouble. It will bring you renewed health, enable you to spend many pleasant hours, save your greengrocer's bill, and generally make your wife, your family, and your home all the brighter and happier.

A Few Words by the Editor

I have special pleasure in presenting this section of the One & All Popular Garden Books, for many reasons. The circumstances under which it is published are full of interest. One of the most earnest and devoted philanthropists of our time, Dr. J. B. Paton of Nottingham, conceived the idea of establishing gardens for our soldiers, who live in barracks where there is generally too little of human interest and variety for their lives, in spite of some excellent recent improvements and developments. This idea he communicated to me, requesting me to co-operate in the good movement, for which he hoped to gain the effective help of Mr Haldane, M.P., our able War Minister. One set of such gardens has been successfully established at Mill Hill Barracks by the active efforts of Major Pemberton. For these gardens our One & All Association furnished seeds and other supplies, and organised a course of lectures to the soldiers on garden-culture bent. The results have fully justified Dr. Paton's anticipations as regards their educational and recreative effects. It can clearly be seen that a general development of gardens of the kind would be a work of national importance.

The two "lectures" prepared for the benefit of soldier-gardeners are so good, so clear, so comparatively complete that I confidently anticipate for them a wide welcome by amateurs of all classes and conditions. Special care has been taken to illustrate fully Mr. Wright's instructions, and to make the two garden books easily understandable by anyone.

Edw.ᵈ Owen Greening

❧ Garden Allotments ❧

A Lecture to Learners

By J. Wright, V.M.S., F.R.H.S.,
Victoria Gold Medallist in Horticulture, Chief County Instructor on
Gardening for the Surrey Education Committee

NEVER before was there such a need and, happily, such a demand for knowledge as exists now on matters of serviceable gardening by the spade workers of the community. Great results have already been achieved in much more than doubling the produce of the soil under tuition and encouragement. Not only may still greater results be confidently expected, but they are bound to be more numerous as the years roll round.

No occupation is more healthful than that of gardening, or more inspiring, when men and youths have learned to love it. They are then never so happy as when on their plots, and these never fail to respond to cultural care by the yield of bountiful crops. Men who have spare hours at disposal and opportunities for spending them on allotments cannot be more creditably, more interestingly, and more profitably engaged – i.e., when by their knowledge, love, and industry they make themselves masters in the art of soil cultivation. Many have done so to their great advantage, but still far more need sound guidance. Can it be afforded by an old soldier who has risen from the ranks of honourable labour and is more than willing to try?

◈ Science and Practice ◈

First, then, though plain matter-of-fact routine is needed by plain and earnest workers, they also ought to know the 'reason why' certain operations should be performed; and, knowing this, they will proceed with greater confidence along the straightest and surest path to the object of their hopes. 'We well know,' wrote a wise man, 'that science points out and illumines the path of the gardener, but the path itself is good practice.' Along that path, and guided by that light, we will travel together for a little while.

◈ A Good Foundation – The Soil ◈

Allotment gardeners and shed, c. 1910

When a man commences to build, his first concern is for a good foundation. So it is in gardening, and we will therefore start at the bottom and work upwards – start with the soil. What is soil? It is the pulverised matter of rocks and varies as rocks vary. It is eventually enriched by the residue of vegetation, which grows and decays. It is this which gives to soil its dark colour, the colouring matter being known as humus, and in due proportion serves an important purpose. In excess it is injurious, yet there is a remedy – lime, which changes to chalk.

Soils differ extremely – one extreme being clay, which represents heaviness; the other extreme being sand, which represents porosity. Blend the two and we have loam. If the clay greatly preponderates we have strong or clayey loam; if the sand much overpowers the clay we have light or sandy soil. Provided that soils can be worked freely, smashed, and pulverised (that being important), the stronger they are the better crops they will grow.

These strong loams or soils are called 'holding' a good 'holding soil' being a common expression, and a scientifically correct one, because the food of plants is literally held in such soils for appropriation by their roots. Sand has no such power, and the food received naturally in the form of rain and atmospheric gases, or artificially in manure, slips through it. That is why sand is poor, and without the addition of clay or heavy soil cannot easily be made rich.

Digging and Trenching

In a book published for amateurs they are told to take out a trench two feet wide and deep, then to turn into the bottom of this trench the top spit of the next two feet in breadth, and from below this to dig out a foot of the fresh subsoil and place it on the other, and so proceed till there is a foot in thickness of this bottom soil, which may have been buried for centuries, all over the piece, the best soil being then a foot under the worst. That is dangerous teaching. In an experiment £80 were spent in trenching a piece of land in that way, and then much expended in manure for making the bad soil grow something; but no good crops were had till the whole piece was trenched over again,

Using cold frames in Aberystwyth, c. 1901

and then the cost incurred was twice as much as the freehold was worth. There are thousands of similar examples on a smaller scale of doing what is really important work wrongly.

The right way is to so dig or trench that only two or three inches of the raw under-soil may be mixed with the better surface soil, breaking up the subsoil and leaving it at the bottom of the trench; and if it can be covered with vegetable refuse of any kind (except deep-rooting weeds), green or decayed, the bad soil will be made better, and more of it can be turned up at the next digging. Never dig ground when it is frozen, covered with snow, nor when the surface treads into a puddle. It would be better to pay a man for resting than for working under these conditions, for digging in ice of necessity lowers the temperature of the soil, and trampling on it when wet squeezes out the air. When the work is done with the greatest ease and comfort to the workman it is done the most efficiently, and it can be done better and easier with forks than spades in heavy soil.

Light porous soils ought not to be manured and dug in the autumn, or the winter rains will wash out the nutriment, and the larder will be comparatively bare by the summer. They should be dug in early spring, and well trodden before cropping, so that the manurial matter applied may be the better retained.

⊰ Seeds and Sowing ⊱

Procure the best possible seeds, and sow thinly – preferably, in drills, in which small seeds should not touch each other. A weak, ill-fed seed cannot produce a robust plant; but remember that good plants cannot be had from the best of seeds by the overcrowding of the seedlings. Practically all vegetables except the onion family and asparagus produce seeds which divide into two lobes or seed leaves. These cannot be too large and strong. If they press against each other the plants are weakened in their infancy – often ruined. Seeds should be sown at a uniform depth for each kind in pulverised soil, not at different depths in cloddy soil. Small seeds are often covered too deeply; very large seeds not deeply enough, as they need more moisture than the smaller kinds. As a rule, very small seeds, such as cabbage, turnip, and others of a similar size, may be covered just under an inch deep; onion, carrot, parsnip, about an inch; radish, spinach, and beet, nearly 2 inches; peas, 3 inches; beans, 4 inches; but all are better sown deeper in summer, when the ground is dry, than in early spring, when it is moist.

❧ Thinning Seedlings ❧

Too thick sowing and too late thinning of seedlings is a double evil by far too common. It means wasting seeds and spoiling plants, besides abstracting nutriment from the soil by those drawn out too late and thrown away. All such as beet, carrots, turnips, parsnips, and others are usually thinned after crowding. Surplus plants should always be drawn out singly from time to time before they touch each other, without disturbing those which are left to become larger.

❧ The Action of Leaves ❧

When the important work that is done by leaves is fully comprehended those vital parts of plants will be more cared for and cherished. With the best seed, soil, manure, and climate in the world, it is not possible for any person to obtain the greatest bulk of the best produce in the absence of sound, strong, clean, healthy leafage of whatever crops he may desire to grow. The leaves are the lungs of plants, and more. They are the breathing, food-manufacturing, and digestive organs of every plant and crop grown in gardens or allotments.

❧ The Duty of Cultivators ❧

Success in gardening is a question of doing all things, especially small things, well, and not too late. Remember the words of a famous General: 'I promote' (said Napoleon) 'those men who are careful in carrying out small details; any elephant can lift a hundredweight; few can pick up a pin.'

❧ Cropping Garden-Allotments ❧

By John Wright, V.M.S.

❧ Vegetable Cropping ❧

In order that the greatest amount of sound information may be compressed into the smallest space, vegetables may, for purposes of cultivation, be arranged in three distinct groups:–

Group I. Bulbous and deep fleshy-rooted kinds.
Group II. Pod and fruit bearing kinds.
Group III. Fibrous-rooting leaf and early tuberous crops.

Why this grouping? The answer is: Because each group should if possible have a change of site every year for at least three years, and possibly more.

❧ Rotational Cropping ❧

Take, say, a 10-rod allotment. For cropping purposes its length, where practicable, should be over thrice the width. All serviceable vegetables could be grown over the area in well-balanced proportions. A rational method of occupying the space would be to run a line through the centre and plant one long half with potatoes – one-third a few rows of first earlies, but still more second earlies, for summer and autumn use; the remaining two-thirds with late varieties for storing for use in winter and till 'potatoes come again.'

The other long half would afford a full supply of all other useful crops, and might be advantageously arranged as indicated in the

Garden plan adopted in Surrey School Gardens

Within the diagram:

ROTATIONAL CROPPING.

End Path.

Broad Beans
(Vegetable Marrows after Radishes)
Peas
(Celery and Leeks after Spinach)
Peas
(Lettuce)
Fr. Beans
(Lettuce)
Fr. Beans
(Savoys)
Potatoes
(Kale)
Potatoes
(Brussels Sprouts)
Early Turnips
(Coleworts)
Early Cabbage
(Lettuce)
Cauliflower
Winter Onions
Spring Onions
Parsnips
Beet (Long)
Carrots (Long)
Carrots (Short)
Beet (Short)
Flowers

End Path

B. PODBEARERS. (to be followed by Fibrous Rooters)

C. FIBROUS ROOTING LEAF AND TUBEROUS CROPS. (to be followed by Deep Rooters)

A. DEEP ROOTING CROPS. (to be followed by Podbearers)

Side Path

Side Path

R = Runner Beans, (at one end only)
S = Shallots, in margin, across rows of Onions.

REFERENCE.
P = Parsley, corner tufts, to arch over Paths.
T = Tomatoes, may rise above flowers.

---

plan (opposite), which is one of many hundreds of boys' instructional 1-rod plots in Surrey.

Intercropping

Besides showing a sound method of 'rotational' cropping, or certain crops following others of different kinds with differing needs, the plan above also suggests examples of 'intercropping' or the growing of certain crops between others, not only without injury, but with advantage under good management.

Take an example with peas (for staking) as the main crop. There is much vacant space between the rows when these are at proper distances. They should be at the least 6 inches further apart than the peas grow in height. Exactly down the centre between the rows a line of spinach may be sown at the same time, and on each side of the spinach radish seed may be scattered thinly. The error to avoid is in leaving spare spinach or radishes to push up tall flower stems to exhaust the soil and exclude light and air from the peas. The point to remember is this: Never let any vegetables remain in the ground after they cease to be useful, as all they can do then is to deprive the soil of its virtues and give nothing in return. The spinach and radishes can in due course be followed by celery, leeks, or vegetable marrows.

Other examples of intercropping are seen on well-managed allotments. Dwarf early potatoes in rows 2 ½ feet apart can be intercropped with savoys, brussels sprouts, kale, and broccoli planted when large enough from seed sown in spring, as these crops do not require the whole of the ground till the potatoes are cleared away.

Vegetable marrow plants are often put in at intervals of 3 or 4 yards between potatoes, and spread over the ground, bearing good crops of fruit if the season is fine, after the potatoes are removed. All that is necessary is to start the plants with a spadeful or two of manure, and the potato tops will afford them shelter after planting at the end of May or early in June.

Profitable crops of scarlet runners can be had after dwarf early potatoes, the beans being dibbled between the potatoes in May, the rows of these being a yard apart. When the runners produce twiners they are chopped off with a sharp knife, and by continuing the practice from time to time the plants are converted into bushes, and bear abundantly. Scores of acres of scarlet runners are made dwarf in that way (not always between potatoes), and grown without sticks for affording tons of pods for market.

The time-honoured plan of dibbling a broad bean in here and there with potatoes, say at intervals of 4 or 5 yards, gives useful crops, stolen, so to say, from the ground, without the potatoes being appreciably injured; indeed, in wet seasons they are benefited rather than other-wise, the beans abstracting moisture which in excess is injurious to the tubers. When that is done a plot

Surrey School Gardens at Benhilton, Surrey

of ground need not be set apart for these beans by persons who desire to grow them.

Another combination may be mentioned. Hardy cos and cabbage lettuce raised by sowing in the open, very thinly, in the first week in September, and the seedlings never allowed to touch each other, may pass through the winter. Planted a foot apart in rows 2 feet asunder in March, there is room between the rows for dwarf French beans at the end of April or early in May. After the lettuces are cleared (pulled up, not cut), green coleworts – a small cabbage – take their place. Then sturdy cabbage plants, raised by sowing about the middle of July, follow the beans in September, and are valuable the following spring.

Deeply worked and well-enriched ground is essential to this close continuous cropping, also after-dressings of soot and chemical manures for inducing free growth. London market gardeners are great believers in soot, and they do not believe in what does not pay. There is, however, a great difference in soot, and a gentleman who was a large buyer of it once bribed a sweep to tell him how to know when it is pure and good. The test is very simple. If a handful cannot be grasped and kept, but flies out between the fingers, it is pure; if it 'cakes' in the hand it is not.

❧ Observations on Vegetables ❧

Broad Beans – Watch for and destroy the first insect; never wait for two. Top the plants when half the flowers open. Early shelter is important. If slugs about use clear lime water an hour after dark.

Dwarf French Beans – Gather the pods when large enough for use (whether used or not), as when seeds form and swell in them flowering ceases and the crop is over all too soon. It should continue for several weeks.

Runner Beans – Insert sticks early, always before the twiners coil; or top them often to make bushes.

Peas – Stake before ½ an inch high with brashy twigs at the base cut from the tallest sticks. Thread against birds.

Beet – Thin early and gradually, watch for and crush the maggot in the leaf blisters. If birds devour the seedlings of the dark leaved, grow the green-leaved sort; the roots are red.

Carrots – Prevent fly-causing maggot, with paraffin in sand or sawdust when the seedlings crack the ground and after. Apply in the evening. In thinning make the soil close, leaving no fissures next the plants to admit the destructive fly.

Parsnips – Thin early and by degrees. Watch for and crush the blister maggot. If dark canker specks appear on the crowns cover them with lime.

Turnips – Paraffin oil in sand or sawdust that will crumble or a wineglassful of the oil in a gallon of strong soapy water sprinkled on in the evening when the germinating seeds crack the soil, and after, will often master the destructive flea-beetle.

Onions – Apply as for turnips early and often, and the smell will drive away the maggot fly. Keep stirring the soap and paraffin mixture. If mildew appears on onions, promptly spray with an ounce of liver of sulphur in three gallons of soapy water.

Cabbage and all plants of a similar nature are often devoured by the flea-beetle. Treat as for turnips. If clubbing occurs cut all small warts off the stems and swirl these and the roots in a puddle of soil, soot, soap-suds and paraffin before planting.

Lettuce – Plants often "bolt" in summer instead of hearting after transplanting. To avert the disappointment in April onwards scatter a few seeds out every fortnight and thin gradually to one in each patch. There will then be no check by transplanting, but probably a succession of good lettuce.

Spinach – Thin early for obtaining large leaves, and let no plants remain to flower, or they will be mere weeds, impoverishing the soil and giving nothing in return.

Radishes – These, when early and tender, are profitable, but can only be so by sowing thinly in rich friable soil. The more crowded the leaves the worse the roots.

Vegetable Marrows – Spindled plants by growing too long under are not so good as sowing two or three seeds over a shovelful or two of good manure worked in the soil, and inserting two or three seeds after the middle of May. Shelter and protect from slugs as needed. The bush marrow affords fruits earlier than the trailing kind.

Tomatoes – As these cannot be safely planted out till June, April is soon enough for sowing seeds for obtaining stout plants under glass. They should be sturdy and thrifty when put out, and even then shelter of some kind may be desirable. Many cottagers have home-made greenhouses and grow excellent crops of tomatoes in them. Some few grow cucumbers also. They require more warmth and moisture, but less ventilation than suit tomatoes.

Potatoes – In earthing leave no sign of a ridge between the rows, but bring all of the soil right up to the stems to form broad round-shouldered ridges. Leaving the plants as if standing in a trough-like channel is a too common mistake; it prevents good crops, as tubers come direct from the stems, and it permits the disease spores to reach those that are not well covered with soil.

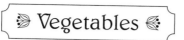

Vegetables

By Horace J. Wright, F.R.H.S.

THERE are, doubtless, some few people still remaining who profess that they cannot see beauty in the vegetable quarters of a garden, but the sensible person sees a twofold charm. A splendidly grown bed of Potatoes, or Cabbages, or Onions is as handsome in its totally different way as a bed of Stocks, or Asters, or a row of Sweet Peas, and it has the additional merit of utility. Indeed, it is a necessity, for without fresh vegetables there are not many among our teeming town populations who would be able to live in that perfect health which alone brings happiness. And the better the culture of the several kinds, and the fresher they can be served upon the table after gathering, the higher will be their nutritive value and the richer will be their flavour. Gradually, but nevertheless surely, the nation is coming to see the full value of vegetables. Hitherto they have been consumed largely as a change from meat, or as an addition thereto, adding to its palatability and its digestibility. But nowadays it is known that the ordinary vegetables of our gardens contain all the essential foods, and that it is not only possible but exceedingly easy for life, and vigorous life too, to be sustained on them alone. Bulk for bulk the meat may show the higher nutritive value, but the foods are in the vegetables, and, properly cooked, they will respond to all the demands that may be made upon them by the human machine. As a matter of fact, there is not the smallest room for doubt that the nation would be for healthier if it consumed more vegetables and less meat.

◈ Asparagus ◈

It is not so very many years ago when it was considered that this was a vegetable suitable only for the extensive gardens of the affluent, but it is now recognised as a plant for all gardens in which space can possibly be found for the beds. There is not the slightest need to have these raised above the ordinary level, as was invariably the custom a while back, for if the ground is deeply and thoroughly dug, vegetable refuse and manure worked into the second spit, Asparagus will thrive splendidly, and with annual attention the beds will remain profitable for an unlimited period. There are two methods by which a start can be made, and each grower must choose the one which is the more convenient to himself. After the preparation of the soil in the early months of the year, the position chosen should be allowed to settle down a little, and one or two-year-old plants purchased expressly for the purpose can be planted 15 in. apart in rows 3 ft. asunder; the best time for this work is towards the end of March or in April, when active growth has just made a start after the winter's rest. By this means we shall have a bed in bearing in the second or third year subsequently to planting, according to the age of the original stock.

◈ Globe Artichokes ◈

These are not nearly as popular at home as they are in France, and it cannot be claimed for them that they are plants for the small garden, as they take up a considerable amount of space which might be more profitably devoted to other crops. They, however, provide a welcome change vegetable for those who can afford the time to eat them. The most suitable soil is a deep, rich, light loam, and propagation can be readily effected from seeds sown in stations 2 ft. asunder in March; this distance will suffice for the first year, but in the second each alternate plant must be removed, as a distance of 4 ft. is necessary to successful results. Some finely sifted coal-ashes ought to be drawn up to each plant, and mulchings with manure are most desirable. In autumn the plants must be trimmed up and have coal ashes heaped round and over the crowns. After three years the plants become unprofitable, and those who require a constant supply should therefore do a little propagation every alternate season, or each season, if desired. The summer growths are sometimes blanched by wrapping straw bands round them, and when these are used it is under the name of Chards; the process of blanching will take about six weeks.

⟐ Carrot ⟐

Among tap-rooted vegetables this ranks in importance with, or even higher than, the Parsnip, and it is essentially a crop upon which it is impossible to devote too much care and attention. The most important of all cultural points to bear in mind is that Carrots must never be grown on land which has just had an application of natural manure,

as this almost invariably leads to the production of wasteful, fanged, and forked roots.

In sowing the seeds, the grower who drops clusters of three or four at distances varying a little with the habit of the variety is wise, for he not only saves seeds and labour in thinning, but considerably reduces the danger from attacks of the dreaded Carrot fly. The drills should be about 1 in. in depth and 10 in. to 12 in. apart, according to the variety. With a view to circumventing the fly, the grower should commence to thin out immediately the seedlings have pushed through the surface, and the soil should always be re-firmed to the plants which remain. Sowing should be done successively through March and April, and a further sowing should always be made in July to yield fresh, sweet, small roots in the autumn and early winter, when it is certain that they will be immensely appreciated. Those who desire to have specially excellent roots for exhibition, and have not a soil that is naturally favourable, adopt the practice of boring holes 2 ft. or so deep, filling these with a compost of loam, leaf mould, and sand, and sowing three seeds in the top of each; when the seedlings show through, and it can be seen which will make the finest plant, the others are removed.

The general crop should be lifted in October or November, and the roots stored in a cellar or shed in alternate layers of fine, dry soil or sand and roots. Here they will keep in splendid condition, and can be used as required.

⟫ Kohl Rabi ⟪

As far as British gardens are concerned this is an unimportant crop, and the amount of space devoted to it should always be strictly limited. It is, however, a very palatable vegetable, and sometimes comes in exceedingly valuable, especially in the event of an unforeseen break in the succession of Turnips. The ground must be deep and in good heart, but over-richness induced by the excessive use of natural manures must be strenuously avoided. The drills should be drawn 15 in. asunder and ½ in. deep, and the seedlings thinned until they eventually stand 15 in. or 18 in. apart, for the plants to grow to perfection. There are purple and green varieties, both of which are of equal excellence. Needless to say, Kohl Rabi is a cattle food of the greatest value.

🌿 Leek 🌿

This relative of the Onion is a plant that is most seriously neglected in the smaller gardens of this country. It is actually one of the hardiest vegetables we have, and a constant supply during the winter months, when fresh produce is never too abundant, should be aimed at by all good cultivators. It is a comparatively easy plant to grow, provided that a deep soil which has been generously enriched with natural manure is at command. The plant demands a long season of growth, and seeds should be thinly sown in a box of light soil in a warm frame in February, and a second sowing made on a warm border in the following month. The seedlings must be thinned out and pricked off into nursery beds according to necessity, as it is imperative to success that they shall never become crowded and drawn, and, further, that they shall never cease to grow, as it appears to be impossible to persuade them to grow out of a check which they have received in the young state.

Prior to planting, it is necessary to take into close consideration the principal object of culture. If the plants are particularly wanted for exhibition, trenches, similar to those for Celery, will have to be cut and have manure placed in and soil above that before planting; but if the plants are wanted exclusively for the home, it will suffice to bore holes 10 in. deep with a blunt-ended dibber, or a broom-handle, drop in the plants, fill the hole with water to settle down the soil, and leave them to grow and blanch themselves, which they will do in a perfectly satisfactory manner.

⊅ Parsley ⊰

This is one of the most important of all the garnishing herbs, and no efforts must be spared to maintain a constant supply of the finest leaves. It is as necessary to prepare the ground well for this crop as it is for Potatoes or Onions, and unless this is done the measure of success will never be full. Cultivate deeply and thoroughly, and incorporate a fair dressing of the finest procurable manure, putting the bulk of it in the second spit or between the top and lower layers of soil. Draw the drills 3/4 in. deep, and sow the seeds very thinly in succession from March onwards. Directly the seedlings are large enough to handle commence thinning, and continue gradually until the plants stand at least 9 in. asunder for development.

☙ Parsnip ❧

As a winter vegetable there are few more popular than this, notwithstanding the fact that its nutritive value is comparatively low, and is commonly still further reduced by the almost universal practice of cutting the root into slices prior to cooking, instead of boiling it whole and thus retaining its full flavour. As far as the preparation of the soil and the sowing of the seeds are concerned, the procedure with this crop is precisely the same as that for Carrots, but there are slight differences in management and detail. The rows for Parsnips should never be closer than 15 in., and thinning must always be done to 10 in. asunder. The times of sowing the seeds differ also, as the present crop is perfectly hardy, and, if desired, seeds may be sown in the autumn; but, as a rule, sowing at the earliest possible moment in the spring, when the weather and the soil are favourable, will bring about quite satisfactory results.

☙ Salsafy and Scorzonera ❧

These tap-rooted crops are not of really substantial value, but as change vegetables for use during the winter they might well be more extensively cultivated. The method of preparation of the soil and management is identically the same as for Carrots, but the seeds should be sown in drill 1 ft. apart at the beginning of April, and the plants must be thinned to 8 in. asunder in the rows.

❧ Seakale ❧

This is a most valuable and palatable vegetable, that is more appreciated when produced, so to speak, out of season than when grown normally in the garden. Although plants can be raised from seeds, the system is not recommended for general adoption, as they are some time before they are of value, and increase is so readily effected by the thong- or whip-like portions of the roots after once a stock has been procured. The soil must be deep and good, and forcing is simple if pots or boxes surrounded by manure are used; or three-year-old crowns can be purchased or raised, and these can be lifted and placed in boxes with a little shallow soil in gentle heat, and they will soon develop produce of excellent quality.

❧ Spinach ❧

This green vegetable ought to be far more extensively cultivated, not on account of its high nutritive value, but because it exercises such an excellent effect upon the blood – as a matter of fact, it is one of the finest purifiers that we can have. It is sometimes thought that Spinach will grow in any position or soil, but it is only when the land is deeply worked and judiciously manured and the plants are thinned out to at least 6 and preferably 8 in. apart in the rows, that the finest leaves are produced. Seeds should be thinly sown in drills an inch deep and 12 in. asunder successively from the middle of February until the middle of August, according to requirements. Poverty of the soil and closeness of the plants leads on to bolting, which causes such trouble in the culture of this crop. Early Giant Thick-leaved is a grand variety for general use.

❧ Vegetable Marrow ❧

Vegetable Marrows are very popular fruit-bearing plants, and they are fully worthy of all the attention that can be bestowed upon them. Their constitution is such that no frost can be withstood, and sowing should therefore be made in frames in March or April, and the plants grown steadily forward in small pots until the end of May, when they are planted out in deep, rich soil. Or seeds may be sown where the plants are to grow at the end of May or early in June, and they will crop splendidly, provided that they are allowed an abundance of space and have water as necessary. For this purpose the Bush varieties are invaluable, as they do not occupy much ground, and fruit earlier than those of rambling habit. For general purpose the Long Green and Long White are admirable, but the Green and White Bush must not be overlooked.

☙ Tomatoes ❧

By W. Iggulden, F.R.H.S.
Horticultural Lecturer to the Horticultural College, Studley.

IT is among amateur gardeners that the greatest number of converts to the tomato 'cult' have been made. Professional gardeners also grow many more than they did in my younger days, say from thirty-five to forty years ago. It is not, however, among their employers that the tomato has gained such a popularity, but rather among the

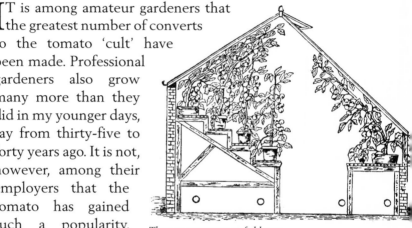

Three-quarter span-roofed house

industrial classes. The rapidly acquired love for tomatoes is really responsible for the remarkable increase in the number of glazed structures to be seen in all directions – these ranging from 'acres of glass,' owned by market growers, to the tiny span-roofed or lean-to structures, of which working-men and amateurs generally are the proud proprietors. It is truly a wonderful revolution, the beneficial effects of which can neither be properly appreciated nor gainsaid. The cultivation of tomatoes affords much pleasurable, and comparatively inexpensive, excitement to innumerable amateurs, and leads to the production of abundance of this wholesome,

132

appetising 'fruit-vegetable.' Tomatoes are come to stay, and are becoming as popular as apples with the man in the street. This is as it should be.

◈ Best Form of House ◈

Which is the best form of house for tomato culture? is a question frequently asked; and I have no hesitation in giving the preference to span-roofed structures. Whether these shall be ten feet, twelve feet, or fourteen feet in width as well as the length, ought to depend upon circumstances, and more especially the means of the intending builder. In either case I would have glazed sides resting on either a light brick wall or boarded substitute – the latter bricks or wood-work – being up to the height it is intended to have side stagings or beds, while the eaves should be from five to six feet above the ground level. The centre, or ridge, should be eight feet to ten feet above the level of door sill, this giving a fair amount of head-room and a moderately sharp roof angle.

The ten and twelve feet wide houses should have side benches or beds only, in width about three feet. In a fourteen feet wide house there may be a bench or bed on each side, thirty inches wide, and a central bed, pit, or staging, four feet wide, which allows for a thirty-inch pathway all round. These span-roofed houses may run in almost any direction, but are most satisfactory when running from north to south. Where there is a sunny wall from four to six feet high that it is desirable should be utilised, a three-quarter span-roofed house, with a five feet high glazed front, may be attached to this; or if the wall be nine feet and upwards in height, that might form a good back to a plain lean-to house, with a front as advised for the other houses. In each and every case both hinged front

How tomatoes are grown at Reading college

and top 'lap' ventilators should be provided, perfect ventilation being essential to success with tomatoes.

Varieties

Each season novelties are introduced, which may or may not be improvements on older varieties. Only those with ample means could give a fair trial to these novelties, and it is a case of the best coming to the front, in the course of time, by sheer merit. Personally, I have found none to excel 'Early Prolific' – a moderately robust, free setting, heavy cropping variety, producing medium-sized and handsome firm fruit of good quality. 'Holmes' Supreme' is another favourite of mine, and this is one of the best for small houses. With the latter I would associate 'The Comet.' These compact-growing, heavy-cropping varieties produce abundance of medium-sized flat-round fruit of the best quality in amateurs' houses. There may be other varieties equal or even superior to those I have named, but I have not met with them. Extra large fruit is not appreciated nowadays, either by judges at flower shows or by connoisseurs generally; but if larger tomatoes for exhibition purposes than those I have recommended are desired, then either 'Perfection' or 'Duke of York' may be grown.

❧ Raising the Plants ❧

For an extra early supply, produced by the aid of a certain amount of forcing, the plants should be raised in September, kept in small pots on shelves in a warm greenhouse till January, and then placed in their fruiting quarters. These should give ripe fruit early in May. As a rule, amateurs will find January, or even February, quite soon enough to commence raising plants,

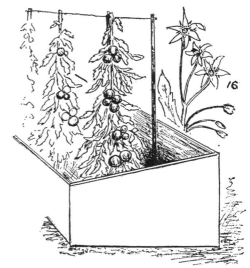

A method of raising tomato plants in frames

and if their houses are largely filled with various greenhouse plants in pots, and not therefore available for tomatoes till early in May, March is the time to sow the seed.

The ingenuity of amateurs is frequently exercised in the matter of 'fixing up' tomato plants in their fruiting quarters. A variety of boxes, tubs, buckets, and the like are requisitioned as being cheaper as well as better in some respects than flower-pots. In pots the soil dries up too quickly, or much more so than it does in non-conductive wooden boxes, shallow tubs, or wooden buckets bought from grocers. These arranged along the fronts or sides of the houses, so as not to interfere with the ventilating irons or gear, hold a row of plants which may be trained fifteen inches or rather less apart. Where there is a central pit or staging, as recommended in the case of span-roofed houses, fourteen feet or more in width, that may also be made to hold two or three rows of plants disposed so as not to unduly shade each other, while the back walls of lean-to and three-quarter span-roofed houses may also be covered thinly with tomato plants.

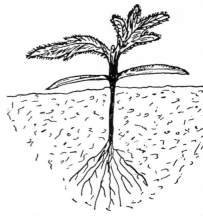

The right depth at which to plant a tomato seedling

❧ Other Cultural Details ❧

Stakes should be placed early to each plant, light ones to conduct them up to a roof trellis of some kind, and much stouter and longer ones for those to be fruited uprightly. In some instances the latter have short stakes placed to each, strings being fastened to these and the roof for the plants to be trained to. I have been advising with the idea that single-stemmed plants only be grown, but if need be a branch or two may be laid in and treated as main stems. Personally, I prefer to keep the plants to one stem, and only recommend the other plan when plants are scarce. No superfluous side-shoots ought to be allowed to develop to a great length before they are cut out, as this means so much wasted energy, and may interfere with the setting of fruit. If the plants grow strongly, continue to train them up the roof or stakes till their limit is reached, though exception should be made in the case of those growing up the roofs of the wider houses, with more tomato plants arranged on the central bed or staging. Topping – that is to say, pinching out the centre of a leader – may be done at one leaf beyond the last truss of flowers.

⚘ Defoliation ⚘

I am making a special paragraph of this, because the system of trimming off nearly all the leaves from tomato plants, directly the lower clusters of fruit are set, seems peculiarly fascinating to amateurs. Carried to the extreme it is however a most senseless, albeit very common, practice, and which I have long fought against. A certain amount of defoliating is necessary in some cases, an instance of which is given by the illustration of a plant where the leaves on the plant were extra strong, smothering most of the fruit. Rows or beds of plants in this condition would be most liable to disease attack. Wholly removing one or two leaves and portions of the rest so as to let air pass through, and to expose the fruit to more light and sun, , is a correct proceeding, and very different to wholesale defoliating. This untimely removal of all the leaves paralyses the growth of the plants, checks the fruit from developing properly, and they are lighter in weight and poorer in quality accordingly.

⇒ Mushrooms ⇐

By R. Lewis Castle, F.R.H.S.,
Superintendent to the Vacant Lands Cultivation Society

AMATEURS commonly regard the cultivation of mushrooms as something beyond their powers, and a kind of horticultural mystery especially reserved to the skill of professional gardeners. It is true a few bold spirits have ventured to undertake the task, but the results have not always been satisfactory to themselves, or encouraging to others who might be disposed to try similar experiments. Yet there are no greater difficulties to overcome than in other departments of gardening, in which amateurs have creditably won conspicuous victories in contests with more experienced rivals.

⇒ The Essentials ⇐

Many useful first lessons in the conditions which govern the growth of mushrooms have been learnt in our fields, where the wild form abounds in early autumn; in fact, several large growers for market attribute their earliest successes to these simple observations. Two of the ruling factors are the temperature and moisture prevailing at the season when these funguses are produced naturally in the open. As soon as the right stage is reached they appear with a magical rapidity; but a sudden change to dry and hot, or cold weather, effectually checks the supplies, and perhaps stops them entirely. Again, apart from the state of air and soil as regards heat and moisture, it is found that some meadows are much more productive of mushrooms than others, which suggests that the quality and character of the soil, the manure present, and the nature or strength of the spawn – the equivalent of the seeds in other plants – have a bearing on the results, a theory in all respects supported by experience.

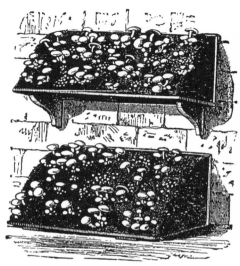

Mushrooms grown on shelves

Here then we have the A B C of mushroom culture, in the imitation by artificial means of natural conditions, which provide suitable moisture and an intermediate temperature, for excessive or deficient heat and moisture are alike inimical, while a sudden extreme change in one direction will arrest growth instantly. A medium, consisting of good soil and manure, is also essential, and added to this the best spawn, which will aid the cultivator in securing the most satisfactory returns for his labour and outlay.

❧ Where can Mushrooms be Grown? ❧

This question might well be put in the form, 'Where can mushrooms *not* be grown?' as the positions suitable for the purpose

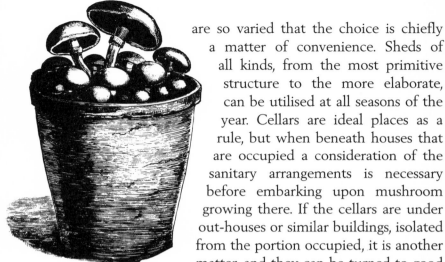

Mushrooms grown in flower pot

are so varied that the choice is chiefly a matter of convenience. Sheds of all kinds, from the most primitive structure to the more elaborate, can be utilised at all seasons of the year. Cellars are ideal places as a rule, but when beneath houses that are occupied a consideration of the sanitary arrangements is necessary before embarking upon mushroom growing there. If the cellars are under out-houses or similar buildings, isolated from the portion occupied, it is another matter, and they can be turned to good purpose. Caves, or excavations in rocky hill sides, are also sometimes at command, and can easily be adapted to the cultivation of mushrooms; while old quarries, or disused surface mines, are equally available in certain districts. Around Paris enormous quantities of mushrooms are produced in old stone quarries. Railway arches have also been extensively employed in the same way.

Lastly, mushrooms can be grown in the open during every month of the year, if the right system be adopted, with the same certainty as under cover. The beds are cheaply and readily formed with the aid of a few boards, and it is possible, where space is too restricted for other methods, to have crops in large pots, tubs, or boxes, which may be purchased for a mere trifle. In fact, there are few gardens or yards in towns, suburbs, or villages where some odd corner could not be utilised in a trial of mushroom culture, and a savoury addition to the ordinary diet obtained at small expense. It must always be remembered, too, that the home-grown samples are free from the doubt respecting wholesomeness as food which not uncommonly attaches to those gathered in the fields and sold in shops or markets.

🐚 Materials Needed 🐚

The only three essential materials are manure, soil, and spawn, but as each of these demands close attention to ensure success, the important points will now be detailed.

Manure – This is indispensable as a source of heat, and to supply a medium in which the mycelium, or spawn, can extend and the mushrooms develop. The most suitable is that from stables where the horses are well fed and littered with straw; peat-moss and other substitutes for the latter are useless to the mushroom-grower. Collections of horse-droppings on macadamised or stone-made roads are suitable if mixed with a good proportion of short litter – say two-thirds of the litter to one of the dung – but manure gatherings from wooden paving, tar, or asphalte are too unreliable to be recommended; while if the roads are newly made or recently repaired the manure is positively dangerous.

Soil – It is usually more difficult for dwellers in and around large cities to obtain good soil than it is to procure the right manure; the tendency, therefore, is to use ordinary garden mould, which, in most instances, is quite unsuitable, for many reasons. The ideal material is that obtained from just beneath the grass in a meadow or good loam, neither very heavy nor extremely light, and where that is not procurable endeavour should be made to secure the nearest approach to it. In any event, let the loam be fresh, and avoid the stale soil of old gardens.

Spawn – The brown dust which is seen under fully grown old mushrooms consists of minute oval bodies termed spores, which perform a function

similar to that of the seeds of flowering plants, though differing in structure and mode of development from them. From these spores is produced the gray or whitish filamentous cobweb-like growths that constitute the "spawn" upon which the majority of modern growers have to rely for the production of mushrooms. In the earlier days this was collected from the fields where the fungus was known to grow naturally, but at the present time it is manufactured on a large scale by specialists who have become noted for their success.

English spawn is commonly sold in the form of flat oblong slabs, termed bricks, which measure 8 to 9 inches long, 5 to 5½ inches wide, and 1¼ to 1½ inches thick. These bricks are composed of manure and soil permeated with the mycelium of the mushroom that has reached a certain stage in its development, in which it can be retained ready for use during several years if carefully stored in a dry, cool place.

A LIST OF THE ONE & ALL GARDEN BOOKS

We have here selected some of the most interesting articles, but there are more to discover! Below is included a list of the original issues.

1. Sweet Peas
2. Annuals
3. Salads
4. Vegetables
5. Perennials
6. Manuring
7. Potatoes
8. Allotments
9. Roses
10. Garden Making
11. Bulbs
12. Weather
13. Onions
14. Climbers
15. Peas
16. Tomatoes
17. Beans
18. Asters
19. Lawns
20. Stocks
21. Pansies
22. Roots
23. Fruit
24. *unknown*
25. Cabbages
26. Small Gardens
27. Garden Allotments
28. Cropping Allotments
29. Mushrooms
30. Phlox
31. Antirrhinums
32. Shady Gardens
33. *unknown*
34. Children's Gardens
35. Small Greenhouses
36. Monthly Reminders
37. Window Gardens
38. Poppies
39. Carnations
40. Indoor gardens

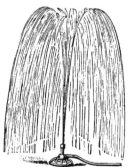

HOLLAND HOUSE
FLOWER SHOW

JUNE 30TH
JULY 1ST
& 2ND

JOHNSON, RIDDLE & CO LTD LONDON S.E.

A beautiful lawn, thickly and evenly grown, free from weeds, obtained and maintained by the yearly use of Velvas Lawn Sand.

Velvas Lawn Sand is a grass food

and weed killer, a lawn beautifier, and a reliable dressing to maintain the grass always in good condition. It gives to the lawn that much sought for, velvet finish in colour and texture. It eradicates all weeds. Apart from the summer enjoyment to be obtained from the possession of a well-grown lawn, there is no part of the garden which figures so prominently in the general ensemble of the garden. And the good lawn is so easy to cultivate. In two or three weeks Velvas Lawn Sand will transform a very ordinary lawn into a beautiful carpet of emerald verdure. Try a tin now. Apply it according to the directions, and note the improvement.

PRICES :—

Tins :—**6**d., 1/-, **2**/-, **3/6**
28lbs., **6/6**   56lbs., **11/-**   112lbs., **20/-**

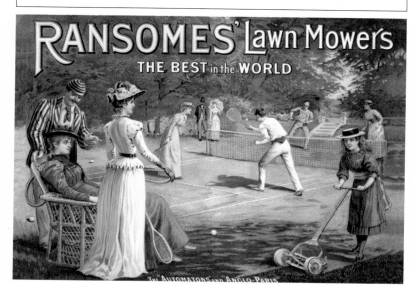

BOULTON & PAUL, MANUFACTURERS.

No. 83. IMPROVED POWERFUL GARDEN ENGINE.

Stott's Sprayers can be attached to this Engine if required.

THE Judges at the great International Horticultural Exhibition held at Manchester tested this Engine very severely, and although all the principal Makers competed, it was declared to be the best, and was awarded the only prize—a Silver Medal.

A Bronze Medal was awarded for this article at the International Exhibition, Hamburg.

The working parts are brass, very simple and easily got at. It has a strong, galvanized iron body, well painted inside and out; wrought-iron wheels with wide tyres, steel spokes, indiarubber delivery pipe and registered spreader; throws a continuous stream.

This Pump will throw water a distance of about 60 feet.

Cash Prices, Carriage Paid.

Width 2 ft. 0 in., to hold 15 gallons		...	£3	0	0
,, 2 ft. 2 in.	,, 20 ,,	...	3	10	0
,, 2 ft. 4 in.	,, 25 ,,	...	4	0	0

Extreme width—15 galls., 25 in. ; 20 galls., 26 in. ; 25 galls., 28 in.

No. 84. THE AMATEUR'S GARDEN ENGINE AND WATER BARROW COMBINED.

THIS Implement will be found very useful in any garden. It is specially suited for Amateur Gardeners, as it can be used for several purposes, viz :—

1st. As a Garden Syringe.
2nd. The Engine can be taken out and used in a pail.
3rd. As a Water Barrow when the Engine is taken out.
4th. For watering lawns, paths, etc., an outlet tap and distributor being provided.

The working parts of the Pump are brass, and will work for years without getting out of order. It throws a continuous stream of water, and is fitted with combined jet and spreader, attached by a universal joint.

Cash Prices, Carriage Paid.

15-gallon size ...	...	...	...	£3	10	0
20 ,, ,, ...	...	...	...	4	0	0
25 ,, ,, ...	...	...	...	4	10	0
		Width same as No. 83.				

JET & SPREADER AS USED WITH ENGINES.

2/6 each.

TESTIMONIALS.

From Mr. J. LUDSBY, The Gardens, Exton Park.

I am highly pleased with the Garden Engine, it is as near perfection as anything I have seen in that way.

From Mr. CHARLES TYLER, Gardener to the Right Hon. the Earl of Wicklow, The Gardens, Shelton Abbey.

I herewith enclose Post Office Order in payment of account for Garden Engine, which pleases me very well.

ROSE CAN BE ATTACHED IF PREFERRED.

Price 2/6 extra.

Carriage Paid on all Orders above 40/- *value to the principal Railway Stations in England and Wales.*